INSIGHTS FOR LIVING LIFE WITH WORTH

KUSHAL GUPTA

This book is fully dedicated to my grandfather,

my brothers,

and to my other family members.

Contents

Contents

Foreword

In a world filled with constant change, growing demands, and ever-increasing distractions, it's easy to feel overwhelmed. Many of us struggle with finding direction, peace, and fulfillment, unsure of where to turn or how to make meaningful progress. In this book, you will find not just inspiration, but practical tools and strategies that can help you navigate these challenges and live a life that is both intentional and rewarding.

What makes this book unique is its grounded approach to personal growth. It doesn't promise a quick fix or magical solution but offers a roadmap for real, sustainable transformation. Every page is a step toward reclaiming your power, strengthening your mindset, and creating lasting change in your life.

The journey you are about to embark on is deeply personal and uniquely yours. Whether you're seeking clarity in your career, healing in your relationships, or simply a deeper sense of purpose, this book provides insights to help you get there. The ideas and exercises presented will not only challenge you but empower you to take charge of your own story and begin writing the next chapter with confidence.

Take your time with this book, and remember: the process of growth is not about perfection. It's about progress, self-compassion, and committing to the person you are becoming.

Now, let's begin this transformative journey together.

— [Saanvi Gupta]

Preface

The true greatness of a person's life is not defined by how long they lived, but by the positive influnce and legacy they leave behind. The value of life is measured in the kindness shown responsibilities fulfilled, and the contributions made for the betterment of others and society as a whole.

Example: Consider Mother Teresa, who dedicated her life to serving the poor and sick.

Her contributions to society were not defined by her age but by her tireless compassion and care for those in need. Even though she lived a humble life, her legacy of kindness and service has had a lasting impact on the world, inspiring countless others to continue her work.

It is not the number of years that define a fulfilling life, but the depth and quality of one's actions. True significance comes from the positive mark one leaves on the lives of others, the duties performed with integrity, and the love and care given freely to family, friends, and community.

Example: Think about someone like Anne Sullivan, the teacher of Helen Keller. Despite facing her own struggles, Sullivan dedicated her life to helping Helen break through the barriers of blindness and deafness. Her patience, dedication, and innovative teaching transformed Helen's life and had a ripple effect, inspiring new methods in education for those with disabilities, Anne's fulfillment didn't come from living a long life, but from the incredible quality and purpose of her work.

Just as a flower blooms only for a short while but fills the world with beauty during its brief existence, a life well-lived is one that brings joy, hope, and inspiration to others, even if it is brief. The essence of a meaningful life is found in the ways one uplifts and touches the lives of others, no matter how short or long their time may be.

Example: Take the story of a young artist who, though they may pass away young, leaves behind a body of work that inspires people for generations. Van Gogh, for instance, did not live a long life, yet his art continues to bring joy, comfort, and inspiration to millions of people worldwide. Like a flower that blooms and fades, his life was short, but its impact has been timeless.

Life's value is not contained within the number of years one lives, but rather in the richness of the experiences shared, responsibilities upheld, and kindness extended to others. A truly meaningful life is a reflection of the impact left on others-the love, wisdom, and guidance offered to family, friends, and community. It is in these selfless acts and the positive ripples they create that the true worth of life is found.

Imagine a candle in a dark room; it may bum only for a few hours, but in that time, it offers warmth and light, brightening the lives of those around it. Similarly, a person's life may be short, yet if they have brought warmth and joy to others, they have lived a fulfilling life. For example, think of doctors who volunteer their time in disaster-stricken areas. They may only be present for a short time, but their presence brings healing and hope to those in need, showcasing that the quality of one's actions is what matters most, not the duration of one's presence.

In this book we don't mean that if a man have money then only he will get respect, instead tis book mean that a man gets respect due to his actions, yah! we have provided a full one part for business and making money because wealth is the most common means in today's world to get respect in society, and many people have mindset that if they will earn the wealth than only they can make their life worth, it's not like that. A man don't get respect due to his wealth, instead he gets respect due to his works and actions.

Example- If there are two types of people. First is a man who have soo much wealth, but if he got all that money because he had robbed a bank, then society will call him theif and he can't get respect in society, maybe people don't tell anything bad about him on his mouth, but I am sure that they will say bad things about him at his back.

Second, there is a person like sir Ratan Tata who had soo much money, but then also he lived a common life, because he donated a huge amount of his wealth to the charities,he worked for society, for people and for his country, due to his this type of action only the people and society respect him.

Today he is not with us, but he will be always alive in our hearts.

Thankyou sir Ratan tata you were such a great personality, and you were the real ratan of our country, about whom no body can say anything ruin .

~Thanykou sir

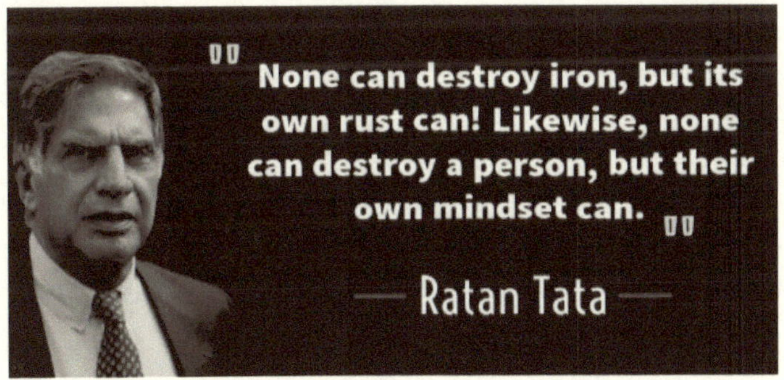

Acknowledgements

Acknowledgments

This book is the product of countless lessons, experiences, and inspirations gathered over the years, and I owe its existence to the remarkable individuals who have enriched my journey.

First and foremost, I want to thank you, the reader, for choosing this book. Your desire for growth, learning, and transformation is the heartbeat of this work. It is for you that I have poured my heart into these pages, and I hope they serve as a beacon of inspiration and guidance.

To my family, who taught me the value of resilience and unconditional love, thank you for your unwavering support. Your belief in me has been my anchor during challenging times and my motivation to keep striving for more.

To my friends and mentors, thank you for sharing your wisdom and for being my sounding boards, critics, and cheerleaders. Your encouragement has been invaluable, and your insights have shaped my perspective in profound ways.

A special thanks to the countless authors, thinkers, and changemakers whose works have inspired me. This book stands on the shoulders of giants who have paved the way for personal growth and empowerment.

Finally, I am deeply grateful to the experiences—both joyous and challenging—that have molded me into who I am today. Each success and failure, every step and stumble, has been a lesson, and I am honored to share these lessons with you.

ACKNOWLEDGEMENTS

May this book serve as a companion in your journey toward a more empowered and fulfilling life. Thank you for allowing me to be part of it.

With gratitude,
[Kushal Gupta]

Rubbish Is Always Rubbish

Keeping your study table free of distractions helps you to maintain focus, just as removing people with negative behaviours from your life keeps you on the path to success.

You should ensure that the human beings which are there in your life, must not have rubbish character, it might be your friends probably, If there is a friend in school who abuses and passes bad comments to anybody, you should maintain distance from him, because he willruin your life as a friend, what you will see that only your mind will capture, firstly you will abhor it but slowlely embrace it and become enfluenced by it.

For example, when men first come into contact with crime, they abhor it. If they remain in contact with crime for a long time, they become accustomed to it and endure it. If they remain in contact with it long enough, they finally embrace it, and become enfluenced by it.

Choose people who lift you higher, not those who drag you down, because you become like the people you spend the most time with, that is why choose wisely

"surround yourself with those who bring out the best in you, not by them who stress you "

whom or what society respects.

The society dosen't honour any person, it honours the position of a person .

For example- If a great businessman is making profit than the people will respect him and always they will speak good about him, but if the time comes that the same businessman facing the losses in his business than the same society and people will disrespect him and speak bad words about him. from this we can understand that the people and society will respect you till you are goging in life and making profits, that is why I always say that there is respect of a person's position not of a person.

Right Is Not Always Right In This Society

You are right to a person till you are according to him, once if he will feel that you are not going according to him then he will say that you are not a good man.... and other rubish things to other people whom he assumes that now also they are according to him, but when he will feel they are also not joining him, again he will repeat the same cycle, because there are excess of humans in this world.

so I suggest you that you should work on making your life worth instead of going back of people that how they will think about you, beacuse its the nature of human that they won't remain at one side for their whole life, in some years , days or sometimes in hours they change their prospective of thinking.

" I AM GOOD FOR YOU TILL I AM ACCORDING TO YOU"

By reading the chapters of this book you will ideas of living life with worth.

PART 1

BEYOND THE PAYBACK : BUILDING THE REAL WEALTH

BEYOND THE PAYBACK : BUILDING THE REAL WEALTH

INTRODUCTION

"PEOPLE SEE ONLY TWO TYPES OF PEOPLEON ROAD ,

ONE WHO IS WITH A LUXURY CAR AND SECOND WHO IS

WALKING WITH NOTHING LIKE BEGGAR "

This observation reflects the contrasting realities that exist within society. It highlights the disparities in wealth, opportunity, and lifestyle. The person with a luxury car symbolizes success, affluence, or perhaps the rewards of hard work and privilege. In contrast, the person walking with nothing can represent struggle, hardship, or simply a different life journey.

Such differences often evoke thoughts about the factors that lead to such disparities-luck, circumstances, choices, societal structures, and opportunities. It serves as a reminder that the paths people take are influenced by a multitude of factors, some within their control and others beyond it.

CHAPTER ONE

YOUR THOUGHTS SHAPE YOUR REALITY

Thoughts are the one of the most powerful things in the world, by thinking you can do many things which are unreachable by the other peoples, how vast you think that much vast you are capable to become, the power of thought plays a crutial role in every field, including business.

Maya had a dream to launch an eco-friendly packing company. Despite her passion, investors dismissed her idea as impractical. Feeling discouraged she visited her grandmother, who said, "YOUR THOUGHTS SHAPE YOUR REALITY".

Determined, Maya visualized her success daily imagining her products on store shelves and customers loving them.

One evening, she met Alex at a networking event, unlike others, he belived in sustainability. Captivated by Maya's vision, he agreed to invest in her startup.

With renewed energy, Maya launched her company. Soon her eco ferendly packing became a hit, inspiring others in the industry. Maya realised that the power of thought had transformed her dream into reality, beliving in her self had opened doors she thought were closed.

By this we understand that when the powerful thought get mixed with burning desire, no one is there to stop you. psychologists have correctly said that "WHEN ONE IS TRUELY READY FOR A THING, IT PUTS IN ITS APPEARANCE", Maya was ready to launch her own company of eco-friendly packing, she remained determined until she got that for which she was seeking for.

she did not said to her self, "AHH, I GUESS IT'S POINTLESS " I'll change my mind and try for something else.

EVERY SETBACK IS ALESSON.

"FAILURE IS NOT OPPOSITE OF SUCCESS IT IS A PART OF SUCCESS"

A frequent reason for failure is tendency to give up when faced with temporary setbacs. You should overpass this type of habit, learn from your mistakes and rejoin again with strong position.

jack was excited to launch his first app, but after months of hardwork, it flopped. Dishearted by the failure he contemplated for giving up. However, he remembered his mentor's advice that "EVERY SETBACK IS A LESSON". Instead of quitting, Jack analyzed the feedback, learned from his mistakes and refined his idea with renewed deternination, he launched the app with improved features . This time, it gained popularity and became a success . Jack realized that failure was not the end, it was merely a stepping stone to his powerful comeback.

The people who embrace a counsciousness of success are the one who ultimately achieve it.

"WINNER ARE NOT THOSE WHO NEVER FAIL"

Reality based inspiration from Sara Blakely.

In 2008, Sara Blakely faced numerous rejections as she tried to pitch her idea for anew type of hosiery that would eliminate panty lines. Despite the setbacs, she remained determined, constantly visualizing her success. Every morning she would repeat affirmations, telling herself that she would create a successful business. With only $5000 in her savings, she developed her product, 'SPANX' and started selling it out of the trunk of her car. Her positive mindset and unwavering belief in her idea attracted attention, leading to a breakthrough when she secured a deal with Neiman Marcus.

Sara'sthoughts and determination transformed her vision into reality. Spanax quickly became a house hold name, making her billionaire and a symbol of entrepreneurial success. She proved that a strong thought or mindset can shape one's reality, even in the competative world of business.

Sara Blakely

CHAPTER TWO

DESIRE AND DREAMS ARE SEEDLINGS OF REALITY

"DESIRE IS THE HEARTBEAT OF EVERY GREAT VENTURE ; IT'S APULSE THAT KEEPS DREAM ALIVE"

Ethan always dreamed of starting his own tech company. He had the skills but lacked the resources and connections . Every night, after his 9to 5 job, he would spend hours in learning about the industry, refining his ideas, and reaaching out to potential mentors. Despite countless rejection and financial setbacks, Ethans desire to build something of his own never wavered .

One day an investor took notice of Ethan's persistence and passion. impressed by his dedication, the investor offered him the fundings he needed. Ethan's company, once just a vision fueled by desire, began to grow. In time, it became a leading name in the tech world.

Reflecting on his journey, Ethan realised that it wasan't luck or talent alone that led him to success- it was his unwavering desire that had transformed his dreams into reality.

Every wish is a fleeting thought that enters your mind, but when you transform that wish into burning desire, it becomes the driving force that leads you to success in any field, encluding business but if you don't convert wish into desire than there is asmall possibility that you will get it

"IF YOU MERELY WISH FOR SOMETHING, YOU MIGHT RECEIVE IT. BUT IF YOU DESIRE SOMETHING WITH ALL YOUR HEART, YOU WILL FIND A WAY TO MAKE IT HAPPEN"

Every successful person achieved greatness by choosing a clear goal and dedicating all their energy, willpower and effort to it. They didn't reach sucess immediately in their chosen fields; instead , they were willing to begin with the most humble tasks, as long as it allowed them to take even a single step towards their cherished goal.

A monumental testament to the strength of the mind is a relentness, burning desire.

Every person who reaches an age where they understand the value of money wishes for it. However, mere wishing will not bring wealth . It is the intense desire for riches, combined with a mindset that turns this desire into an obsession, along with clear plans and relentless persistence that refuses to acknowledge failure , that ultimately leads to prosperity.

The process of transforming a desire for wealth into its financial equivalent involves five key steps .

- You must clearly define the excact amount of money you wish to attain. It is not enough to simply say, " I WANT LOT OF MONEY ."(There a psychological reason for defiteness).
- Clearly define what you plan to in exchange of the money you wish to receive. (There is no such reality as something for nothing).In my voew, it's often necessary to step outside your comfortable zone to achieve the money and success you desire.
- set a specific dateline by which you intend to achieve the financial goals you desire .
- formulate a clear plan to pursue your goals and start implementing it immediately, regardless of whether you feel fully prepared.
- Read your written desire you want to achieve out loud twice a day ;once in the morning after you wake up and once at night before you go to bed. As you read, visualise, feel and believe that you already have the money you desire.

Only those become "MONEY CONSCIOUS" ever accumulate great riches. "MONEY CONSCIOUS" means that the mind has become so throughly saturated with the desire for money, that one can see one's self already in possession of it. If you do not see great riches in your imagination, you will never see them in your bank balance. We who are in this race for riches, should be encouraged to know that this changed world in which we live is demanding new ideas, new ways of doing things, new leaders, new inventions, new methods of teaching, new methods of marketing, new book, new literature.

Tolerance and an open mind are essential for today's dremers; those who fear new ideas are destined to fail from the outset. The world is filled with an abundance of oppertunity which the dreamers of the past never knew, the world no longer scoffs at the dreamers, nor calls them impractical. there is a difference between wishing for a thing and being ready to achieve it.

EVERY FAILURE BRINGS WITH IT THE SEED OF AN EQUIVALENT SUCCESS"

~Napoleon hill

THE POWER OF DESIRE : INSPIRATION FROM HOWARD SCHULTZ

The story of Howard Schultz and Starbucks is a prime example of how the power of desire can shape the future of a business. In 1982, Schultz, who had a background in sales, joined Starbucks, a small coffee bean retailer in Seattle. At the time, Starbucks was just selling high-quality beans, with no focus on brewed coffee or café culture. However, Schultz's desire to create something more than just a place to buy beans began to take shape during a trip to Italy, where he was inspired by the vibrant coffeehouse culture.

In Italy, Schultz saw how cafés were not just about coffee but about community, social connections, and an experience. He believed this concept could be replicated in the U.S. His desire was to bring that Italian coffeehouse experience to American consumers by offering high-quality coffee, a welcoming environment, and a place for people to gather.

When Schultz pitched his idea to the company's founders, they were initially resistant, believing that serving coffee was outside their core business. But Schultz's unwavering passion and desire to bring his vision to life led him to buy the company in 1987 for $3.8 million.

Schultz's vision transformed Starbucks from a small, local Seattle business into a global coffee empire. He expanded the company by opening stores not just in the U.S. but eventually across the world, creating a new coffeehouse culture that centered on a unique customer experience. Starbucks became more than just a coffee shop—it was a "third place" between home and work, where customers could relax, work, or socialize.

Schultz's desire to create a company with a deep sense of community and social responsibility also played a role in Starbucks' success. He made sure that employees, or "partners" as they are called, received benefits such as healthcare and stock options, a unique offering in the service industry.

Today, Starbucks is a global brand with thousands of stores worldwide, and Schultz's story demonstrates how a deep desire to change the way people experience coffee, combined with relentless determination, can turn a small idea into a global phenomenon. His journey shows that with a clear vision and a strong desire to make a difference, it's possible to reshape an entire industry.

Remember that all who succeed in life get off to a bad start, and pass through many heartbreaking struggles before they "ARRIVE".

Howard Schultz

CHAPTER THREE

LIGHT IN DARKNESS: THE GUIDUING POWER OF FAITH

"A MAN OF FAITH WILL REMAIN STEADFAST AND WILL GO ON PERFORMING HIS DUTY, EVEN IF THERE IS NO OTHER OUTCOME IN SIGHT"

~ MAHATMA GANDHI

Faith in business refers to the belief and trust in one's vision, goals, abilities, and the process, even when the outcome is uncertain or the path ahead is unclear. It involves having confidence that hard work, dedication, and the principles guiding the business will eventually lead to success, despite challanges, setbacks, or external factors.

This kind of faith inspires resilience, preservance, and a positive mindset, which are crucial for navigating the unpredictable nature of the business world.

Raj had always dreamed of starting his own coffee shop, but he hesitated for years, fearing failure. One day, he decided to take a leap of faith and rented a tiny space in a busy neighbourhood. with all his savings invested, Raj poured his heart into creating a cozy atmosphere and brewing the best coffee he could.

The first month was rough - barely any customer came in. Friend suggested that he should cut his losses and move on, but Raj refused. He believed that if he stayed true to his vision, success would follow him.

One rainy afternoon, a local journalist seeking shelter wandered into Raj's shop. Impressed by the warmth and unique flowers, she wrote an article praising his coffee. The next day, Raj's shopwas filled with curious customers eager to try the coffee they had read about.

Raj's business flourished from that day. Looking back, he realised it wasn't luck that made his dream come true- it was the unwavering faith he had in his vision, even when no one else could see it.

" HOW TO CULTIVATE UNSHAKEABLE FAITH".

The principal of auto- suggestion plays a crucial role in transporting desire into tangible outcomes, such as financial success. essentially, faith can be cultivated or established by consistently affirming or repeating messages to the subconcious mind. This process of auto- suggestion allows individuals to influence their mental state, thereby facilitating the realization of their goals and aspiration.

Developing faith where it dosen't exist can be very challanging to explain. It's similar to trying to describe the colour blue to someone who is blind and has never seen colours before; he have no reference point to understand what you mean.

HOW TO EXPLAIN THE CONCEPT OF FAITH TO SOMEONE WHO HAS NEVER EXPERINCED IT.

To explain faith to someone who has never experinced it, emphasize that faith is trust and confidence in something not seen.It involves bwleiving in promises or truths without direct evidence, similar to trusting a friend to keep a thing secret.

Biblical defination describe faith as the assurance of things hoped for and the evidence of things not seen.(Hebrews 11:1)

Using relatable examples, like believing in future outcomes or relying on someone's word, can help to illustrate how faith operates in daily life, when tangible proofs is lacking.

DIFFERENT RELIGIONS DEFINING THE FAITH.

- HINDUISM AND BUDDHISM - Faith often involves trust in spritual teachers or gurus rather than singular diety. Concepts like devotion (Bhakti) and compassion (Karuna) are emphasized over faith in god.
- JUDAISM - Faith is linked to adherence to god's convenant and truthfulness of promises made between

God and Israel (A reference to a people chosen by God) reflecting a juridical aspects.

- CHRISTIANITY - Faith is a divenly inspired trust in god, rooted in the historical revelation of Jesus Christ. It is often described as gift from god.
- Islam - Faith is central to a believer's identity, defined as trust in god and his will.It is believed that true faith can only be attained through God's will.

HOW CAN ENTREPRENEURS INTEGRATE FAITH INTO THEIR BUSINESS STRATAGIES.

1. Enrepenures can integrate faith into their business ideas, before god asking for eisdom and direction to align decisions with devine purpose.
2. OPERATE ON BHAGVAT GITA PRINCIPLES - Establish a business culture that reflects values like integrity, humanity, and service ensuring that ethical consideration guides all decision.
3. VISUALIZE SUCCESS - Use faith to envision achieving business goals, beleiving in success before it manifests. This helps to maintain motivation and clarity in decision making.
4. EXERCISE PATIENCE - Trust in God's timing for oppertunities, avoiding hasty decision. Faith encourages perseverance through challanges.
5. EMBRANCE COMMUNITY - Engage with like - minded individuals or groups to foster a supportive enviroment where faith - driven entrepreneurialism can thrive.

IMPORTANCE OF FAITH IN BUSINESS : INSPIRATION FROM FRED SMITH, FOUNDER OF FED EX.

Faith in business plays a crucial role in navigating challenges, making decisions, and fostering growth. Fred Smith, the founder of FedEx, exemplifies how faith, both in one's vision and in people, can drive a business to success. Here's how faith has influenced Fred Smith's journey with FedEx:

1. Faith in the Vision

Fred Smith's belief in his vision for FedEx was a driving force behind the company's early struggles and ultimate success. In 1971, Smith launched FedEx with a revolutionary concept: an overnight delivery service that would guarantee shipments could be sent anywhere in the world within 24 hours. At the time, this was an audacious idea, and many were skeptical. His unwavering faith in this vision, despite initial challenges—including a critical $29 million loss in the early years—allowed him to push through obstacles. Smith's belief in innovation, customer service, and reliability helped shape FedEx into a global logistics leader.

Key Takeaway: Faith in your vision can be a powerful catalyst for overcoming difficulties. Even when faced with skepticism or adversity, having a clear vision and confidence in your idea helps you stay focused and resilient.

2. Faith in People

Smith has always emphasized the importance of the people who work at FedEx. He believed that creating a strong company culture, where employees are treated as valued stakeholders, is vital for long-term success. Fred Smith often said that FedEx's most important assets were its people, and he was committed to ensuring that they were well taken care of. By giving employees opportunities to grow, and by fostering trust and respect, Smith built a company culture that values service, accountability, and teamwork.

Key Takeaway: Faith in your team and creating an environment of trust and respect leads to motivated, loyal employees who contribute to the overall success of the business. When leaders believe in their people, those people are more likely to believe in the company's mission.

3. Faith in Perseverance and Innovation

Fred Smith's faith also extended to his belief in perseverance and continuous innovation. Despite setbacks, including financial hardships and regulatory hurdles, Smith maintained his belief in the power of technological advancement and service excellence. FedEx introduced systems such as real-time tracking and automated sorting, which transformed the logistics industry. His faith in the importance of technology and his ability to anticipate future needs helped FedEx evolve and adapt to changing times.

Key Takeaway: Perseverance, paired with an openness to innovation, is essential for navigating the unpredictable nature of business. By continually evolving and staying ahead of industry trends, businesses can remain competitive and relevant.

4. Faith in Ethical Leadership

Fred Smith's leadership was rooted in strong ethical values. He believed that integrity, honesty, and transparency were fundamental to maintaining trust with customers, employees, and shareholders. This faith in ethical leadership played a role in FedEx's enduring reputation as a reliable and trustworthy brand.

Key Takeaway: Business leaders should hold themselves to high ethical standards. Ethical conduct helps build long-term relationships, enhances reputation, and ultimately strengthens the company's brand.

Conclusion

Fred Smith's faith in his vision, people, perseverance, innovation, and ethics has been key to FedEx's growth and success. He showed that faith, when combined with hard work, innovation, and leadership, can create a thriving business. In today's business world, having faith in these core principles can still provide the inspiration needed to overcome challenges and achieve lasting success.

FRED SMITH

CHAPTER FOUR

THE CREATIVE CATALYST: HOW IMAGINATION DRIVES BUSINESS SUCCESS

" IMAGINATION IS MORE IMPORTANT THAN KNOWLEDGE".

~ Albert Einstein

Imagination is the creative workshop of the human mind, where every plan and idea takes shape. It is driven by desire and brought to life through the dynamic force of action. Anything that the human mind can conceive, it has the power to create.

In today's world, more than any other period in history, we have an unparalleld oppertunity to nuture and expand our imagination. The constant exposure to new ideas and rapid changes around us provides endless inspiration for developing this vital skill.

with the power of imagination, humanity has achieved extraordinary feats in recent times, harnessing more natural forces than ever before. we've mastered the skies, developed instant global communication, and even explored the vastness of space. imagination is enabling us to decipher the mysteries of the universe, showing that our minds are capable of both transmitting and receiving the energy of thought, opening doors to limitless possibilities.

TWO FORMS OF IMAGINATION.

In "THINK AND GROW RICH ", Napoleon Hill discusses two primary forms of imagination : synthetic imagination and creative imagination.

lets dive deep into each.

1. Synthetic Imagination

Synthetic imagination is the ability to take elements of existing ideas, concepts, and knowledge, and rearrange, combine, or adapt them into new forms. This form of imagination does not create something entirely new, but rather offers a way to innovate and improve upon what already exists. It is primarily a process of "recombining" and "restructuring" familiar components to form a new or more effective solution.

Characteristics of Synthetic Imagination:

Building on the Existing: This form of imagination is rooted in the tangible and the familiar. It operates within the constraints of what is known and makes improvements or adaptations based on that knowledge. Think of it as the art of combining or altering existing ideas and innovations to create something novel or more efficient.

Problem-Solving and Innovation: Synthetic imagination is highly practical and is often used by entrepreneurs, business leaders, and inventors to solve problems or make improvements. This is the type of imagination that allows someone to see a gap in the market and devise a way to fill it by improving existing products or services.

Efficiency-Oriented: Rather than groundbreaking invention, synthetic imagination focuses on efficiency and practicality. It's about figuring out ways to take what's already been created and make it better, faster, or more relevant to current needs.

Example of Synthetic Imagination:

A classic example of synthetic imagination can be seen in the evolution of the smartphone. The smartphone didn't arise from an entirely new concept but rather was the result of combining existing technologies—mobile phones, personal computers, cameras, GPS devices, and touchscreens—into a single, more powerful, and versatile device. Steve Jobs, in particular, used synthetic imagination when he helped develop the iPhone by merging the features of previous technologies in a completely new way.

Applications in Business:

Product Improvement: A company may take an existing product, like a traditional vacuum cleaner, and redesign it with a more efficient motor, better filtration system, or a more user-friendly interface.

Process Optimization: A business leader might use synthetic imagination to improve a company's workflow, combining best practices from different industries to create a more efficient production line.

Market Expansion: A marketer might adapt a product or service to a different demographic by taking elements of the original product and tailoring them to meet the needs of a new audience.

2. Creative Imagination

Creative imagination is a more profound and abstract form of imagination, which Hill describes as the ability to think outside the box and generate entirely new ideas that have never existed before. This type of imagination connects to the subconscious mind, drawing upon instincts, inspiration, and creativity to bring forth ideas that challenge the status quo and have the potential to revolutionize industries, societies, and even the world itself.

Characteristics of Creative Imagination:

Originality and Innovation: Creative imagination is all about original thought. It is the mental faculty that allows a person to imagine things that have never existed before. It is highly visionary and can lead to the creation of entirely new products, services, industries, or even entirely new ways of thinking.

Intuition and Insight: Unlike synthetic imagination, which works with known ideas, creative imagination taps into a more intuitive and subconscious realm. It's not about logical problem-solving; it's about envisioning new possibilities that often defy logic or conventional thinking. It requires openness to the unknown and a willingness to explore concepts that are not yet proven or tested.

Breakthrough Thinking: Creative imagination often leads to revolutionary ideas and breakthroughs. It is responsible for the creation of things that have never been done before. Many of the world's most transformative inventions or advancements began as an exercise in creative imagination.

Example of Creative Imagination:

One of the most famous examples of creative imagination is Thomas Edison's invention of the electric light bulb. While other inventors had worked with electricity, Edison used creative imagination to visualize and eventually create a practical, mass-producible light bulb that changed the world. Edison didn't just combine existing technologies—he completely redefined how electricity could be used in everyday life. Similarly, the creation of the personal computer, which led to the rise of companies like Apple and Microsoft, is a product of creative imagination, envisioning a future where people could have a computer in their home or office.

Applications in Business:

Inventing New Products: Creative imagination is at the heart of technological breakthroughs. For instance, the creation of the Internet and Google were born out of creative imagination—completely new ways of thinking about communication and information sharing.

Business Models: Innovating new business models, such as the sharing economy model used by companies like Uber and Airbnb, comes from creative imagination. These companies didn't simply tweak existing industries; they reinvented how services could be delivered.

Revolutionizing Industries: Creative imagination is what enables entire industries to be transformed. Elon Musk's vision for electric vehicles and space travel is an example of using creative imagination to radically change the transportation and aerospace industries.

Conclusion: The Power of Both Forms of Imagination

In Think and Grow Rich, Napoleon Hill emphasizes that both synthetic and creative imagination are essential tools for personal and business success. While synthetic imagination allows individuals to build upon and improve existing ideas, creative imagination enables true innovation by generating entirely new concepts and possibilities.

Entrepreneurs and leaders must understand when to use each type of imagination. Synthetic imagination is particularly useful when looking to solve practical problems, improve processes, or adapt to existing markets. In contrast, creative imagination is crucial when seeking to change the game entirely, invent new solutions, or create new industries.

To achieve lasting success, it's important to cultivate both forms of imagination. By combining creativity with practical problem-solving, individuals can unlock the full potential of their ideas and drive both incremental and revolutionary change in their businesses and lives.

six key points fostering a culture of imagination in companies.

1. Encourage Open Dialogue and Idea Sharing

To cultivate a culture of imagination, it's essential to create an environment where open communication is encouraged. Employees must feel safe to share their ideas, no matter how unconventional or unrefined they may seem. When ideas flow freely across all levels of the organization, it creates fertile ground for creativity to thrive.

Action Steps: Establish regular brainstorming sessions where everyone can contribute ideas. Implement an open-door policy that allows employees to approach leadership with their thoughts. Create platforms, both online and offline, where ideas can be shared and refined collaboratively.

2. Provide Time and Space for Creative Thinking

Imagination requires room to breathe. Employees need time to step away from their daily tasks and dedicate themselves to exploring new ideas and thinking outside the box. When employees are under constant pressure to meet deadlines, creativity often takes a backseat. By offering time and physical space for creative thinking, companies allow imagination to flourish.

Action Steps: Dedicate a certain number of hours each week for employees to work on personal projects or innovation. Create quiet, inspiring workspaces or common areas designed to stimulate fresh thinking. Offer flexible schedules that give employees time to think, explore, and experiment.

3. Support Experimentation and Embrace Failure

Imagination often requires risk-taking and experimentation, which can sometimes lead to failure. To foster a culture of imagination, leaders must encourage employees to take risks and view failure as a necessary step toward growth and innovation. Embracing failure as part of the creative process helps employees feel empowered to try bold, new ideas.

Action Steps: Establish a "fail-forward" culture where employees are encouraged to experiment and learn from their mistakes. Reward calculated risk-taking and share stories of failures that led to eventual breakthroughs. Implement pilot programs or small-scale testing of new ideas to mitigate the risks of failure while encouraging creativity.

4. Promote Cross-Disciplinary Collaboration

One of the most powerful ways to foster creativity is by bringing together diverse perspectives. Collaboration across departments and disciplines sparks new ideas that wouldn't emerge in siloed work environments. When individuals from different backgrounds and areas of expertise come together, they bring new ways of thinking and problem-solving, which enhances creative output.

Action Steps: Form cross-functional teams to work on projects, encouraging members from different departments to collaborate. Organize workshops or creative labs where employees from diverse fields can solve common problems together. Ensure that leadership values diverse perspectives and promotes inclusion across the organization.

5. Invest in Continuous Learning and Development

A culture of imagination thrives in an environment where employees are continually learning and expanding their skills. Creativity is fueled by knowledge, new experiences, and exposure to fresh ideas. Companies that invest in training, personal development, and external learning opportunities create an ecosystem where employees are equipped to think imaginatively and apply new knowledge to their work.

Action Steps: Offer access to courses, workshops, conferences, and seminars that foster creativity and innovation. Support employees in exploring new subjects or developing new skills, even outside their core job functions. Encourage employees to pursue side projects or hobbies that might inspire new ideas for the company.

6. Recognize and Reward Creativity

To ensure that a culture of imagination becomes deeply ingrained, it's vital to recognize and reward creative contributions. Public acknowledgment of innovative ideas not only celebrates individual achievements but also reinforces the value of creativity throughout the organization. When employees see that creative thinking is rewarded, they are more likely to engage in imaginative problem-solving.

Action Steps: Create formal recognition programs to highlight employees who demonstrate innovative thinking. Offer incentives such as bonuses, promotions, or public recognition for creative ideas that have a positive impact on the company. Share success stories of imaginative breakthroughs in company newsletters or meetings to inspire others.

Conclusion

Fostering a culture of imagination in your company requires intentional effort across multiple areas: encouraging open dialogue, allowing time and space for creative thought, embracing failure as part of the process, promoting cross-functional collaboration, investing in continuous learning, and recognizing creativity. By embedding these practices into the fabric of your organization, you create an environment where imagination is not just encouraged but celebrated—leading to greater innovation and long-term success.

IMAGINATION : INVENTOR OF STICKY NOTES, DR SPENCER SILVER AND ARTHUR FRY.

In 1968, Dr. Spencer Silver, a scientist working at 3M, was conducting research aimed at developing a super-strong adhesive. However, in an unexpected twist, he invented a low-tack adhesive that was not sticky enough to be used for strong bonding, but still adhered to surfaces without leaving a residue. Initially, Silver thought the adhesive might have practical applications in the aerospace industry, but it didn't meet the necessary criteria for that field. Despite the apparent failure, Silver's imagination led him to keep exploring the possibilities of this unusual material.

Rather than seeing his invention as a setback, Silver used his creativity to envision new uses for the adhesive. This is where imagination played a crucial role—seeing potential where others saw only an error.

Arthur Fry's Creative Solution: Turning Imagination into Reality

In the mid-1970s, Arthur Fry, a colleague of Silver's at 3M and a choir singer, found himself struggling with the small pieces of paper he used to mark his hymnal pages during church services. The paper would constantly fall out, frustrating him. One day, Fry remembered Silver's low-tack adhesive and saw an opportunity to solve his problem. He imagined a sticky note—something that could adhere to paper without damaging it, yet be easily removable.

Fry began experimenting by applying Silver's adhesive to small pieces of paper, and the result was the creation of what we now know as Post-it Notes. Fry's imagination transformed a minor inconvenience into a revolutionary product.

The Breakthrough and Commercial Success

After developing the prototype, Fry and Silver worked together to convince 3M to bring the product to market. However, the road to success wasn't immediate. Initial market testing showed limited success, and the product was slow to gain traction. It wasn't until a bold and imaginative marketing campaign was launched in 1980—featuring Post-it Notes prominently in office environments—that the product exploded in popularity. Consumers saw the potential in the notes, not just for personal use but in the business world as well.

The product's success was a direct result of Silver's original imaginative idea and Fry's ability to recognize its practical application. Sticky Notes became a global phenomenon, transforming office productivity and becoming an everyday staple for millions of people.

Key Takeaways: The Power of Imagination

The invention of Sticky Notes by Dr. Spencer Silver and Arthur Fry illustrates how imagination can turn an unexpected discovery into a groundbreaking product. Silver's ability to reframe his "failure" as an opportunity and Fry's creative thinking transformed a simple adhesive into a tool that changed the world of organization, communication, and productivity.

This story underscores that imagination doesn't always require a sudden eureka moment; it often comes from seeing possibilities in unexpected places and daring to explore them further. The partnership between Silver and Fry is a testament to how creativity, collaboration, and the courage to pursue unconventional ideas can lead to world-changing innovations.

Spencer Silver

Arthur Fry

CHAPTER FIVE

MASTERING THE MINDSET OF SALES

Sales is much more than a transactional process. It is an art, a skill, and above all, a mindset. Behind every successful salesperson lies a mental framework that allows them to navigate the highs and lows of the profession with confidence, resilience, and a drive for continuous improvement. Mastering this mindset is not only the key to success in sales—it's the difference between average performance and exceptional results.

Whether you are just beginning your sales career or are a seasoned professional looking to refine your approach, understanding and mastering the mindset of sales can significantly enhance your effectiveness, build lasting relationships with clients, and propel your career forward. In this chapter, we will explore the core elements that comprise the sales mindset and how to develop them to excel in the field.

1. Embrace Resilience and Rejection

Rejection is part of the sales process. If you're not hearing "no" occasionally, you might not be pushing hard enough or exploring new opportunities. Successful salespeople understand that rejection is not a reflection of their personal abilities, but rather an integral aspect of the journey toward success. In fact, the most successful salespeople see rejection as a learning opportunity—an essential part of the growth process.

The Power of Resilience: Sales requires a mindset shift where rejection is no longer a negative outcome but a necessary part of the path to success. It's how you respond to rejection that matters. Resilience is the ability to quickly bounce back from setbacks and keep going with the same enthusiasm and determination as before. Developing this resilience helps salespeople stay motivated despite the inevitable "no" responses.

Key Thought: Rejection is an opportunity for improvement, not a reason to quit. Every "no" brings you one step closer to a "yes."

ACTION TIP: After facing rejection, ask yourself reflective questions: Why didn't this lead close? Were there areas where I could have better communicated the value of the product? What can I learn from this rejection that I can apply next time? By making rejection part of your growth process, you maintain motivation and keep improving.

2. Cultivate Empathy and Active Listening

Sales are not simply about presenting your product or pushing a deal. The best salespeople are those who take the time to truly understand their prospects and customers. When you approach sales with empathy, you prioritize solving problems rather than pushing a solution. You focus on understanding the needs, desires, and pain points of your customer, which allows you to tailor your sales approach to meet those specific needs.

Active Listening: The Art of Understanding Active listening is the cornerstone of empathy. It means listening not just to respond but to understand. This requires your full attention—no interruptions, no distractions. You must listen to both what your customer is saying and what they are not saying. You must pay attention to tone, body language, and even silences, as these are often as revealing as the words themselves. Only then can you respond with the solutions that will truly resonate with them.

Key Thought: When you focus on understanding your customer deeply, sales become a conversation, not a pitch. The more you listen, the better your solution will be.

ACTION TIP: Practice active listening in your next client interaction. Before responding to any objection or question, pause to reflect on what your prospect is truly saying. Ask follow-up questions that encourage them to elaborate and dig deeper into their needs. This approach builds rapport and trust, which are critical to any sales relationship.

3. Adopt a Growth Mindset

One of the most important elements of the sales mindset is the growth mindset—the belief that you can improve through dedication and effort. Rather than seeing skills as fixed, the growth mindset encourages the view that with practice, feedback, and continuous learning, you can constantly improve and overcome challenges. This mindset is especially vital in sales, where success is not just about closing one deal, but about constant refinement and adaptation.

Continuous Improvement: A growth mindset allows salespeople to see every situation as a chance to learn, whether it's a difficult negotiation, an unsuccessful pitch, or an unexpected objection. By viewing these experiences as stepping stones to growth, you remain open to learning from every opportunity, which accelerates progress and mastery in sales.

Key Thought: Success in sales is a result of continuous learning and adaptation. Every experience provides a valuable lesson that makes you a better salesperson.

ACTION TIP: Identify one area in your sales approach that you'd like to improve—whether it's mastering cold calls, handling objections, or closing deals. Dedicate time to training, reading, or practicing specific techniques in that area. Then, put those skills into action and reflect on what you've learned, repeating the process for consistent growth.

4. Confidence is Key

Confidence is the bedrock of successful sales. A confident salesperson instills trust and belief in their product, service, and themselves. Customers are drawn to confident individuals because they inspire confidence in the product being offered. Confidence, however, isn't about being brash or overbearing. It's about believing in your product's value and having the conviction to share it with others.

Building Confidence in Sales: Confidence comes from preparation, product knowledge, and experience. The more you understand your product, its benefits, and how it fits into your customer's world, the more natural your confidence will become. When you can articulate the value of your product clearly and passionately, customers will feel your certainty—and it will influence their decisions.

Key Thought: Confidence is the belief in your ability to provide value. When you believe in yourself and the product you're offering, you create an environment where customers are more likely to say "yes."

ACTION TIP : If you struggle with confidence, start small. Review your product's features and benefits until you can speak about it naturally. Role-play sales conversations with colleagues to gain more comfort in presenting your solution. The more you practice, the more confident you'll become in real-life situations.

5. Stay Focused on Long-Term Relationships, Not Just Transactions

Sales is often viewed as a one-time transaction. However, the best salespeople view every deal as the start of a long-term relationship. They aim to provide value to their customers long after the initial sale, creating a foundation of trust, satisfaction, and loyalty. Building long-term relationships is not just good for business; it creates opportunities for repeat sales, referrals, and brand advocacy.

Relationship Building: Rather than chasing after the next deal, focus on nurturing existing customer relationships. Show genuine interest in your clients' success, and be there to offer support, solutions, and guidance. By positioning yourself as a trusted advisor, not just a salesperson, you become indispensable to your clients.

Key Thought: Every sale is an opportunity to build a relationship. Satisfied customers are more likely to return and refer others to you.

ACTION TIP: After closing a sale, don't disappear. Follow up with your customers to ensure they're satisfied with their purchase. Offer additional support or resources that might help them, and look for ways to continuously add value.

6. Be Passionate and Enthusiastic

Passion and enthusiasm are the most contagious qualities a salesperson can possess. Customers are more likely to engage with you if they can feel your energy and excitement about the product. Enthusiasm shows that you believe in your product, and when you express that belief authentically, your prospects will trust that you are offering something valuable.

The Power of Enthusiasm: People are drawn to those who exude positivity and excitement. When you speak passionately about your product, customers feel energized, and this emotional connection helps them envision how your product fits into their own lives.

Key Thought: Enthusiasm is infectious. The more excited you are about your product, the more excited your customers will be.

ACTION TIP: Infuse your sales presentations with genuine excitement. When discussing the product, focus on the aspects you're most passionate about. Share your enthusiasm in a way that helps your prospect feel the value you see in the solution you're offering.

Conclusion: Mastering the Mindset of Sales

Mastering the mindset of sales is about more than just skill acquisition—it's about adopting a way of thinking that enhances your approach to every part of the sales process. Resilience, empathy, confidence, relationship-building, and enthusiasm are all crucial aspects of the sales mindset that enable you to connect with customers, overcome challenges, and continuously grow in your profession.

Sales is an ongoing journey of improvement. The most successful salespeople are those who embrace each challenge as a learning opportunity, constantly refine their techniques, and maintain a deep belief in the value they bring to their customers. By adopting this mindset and committing to personal growth, you'll not only become a more effective salesperson but also unlock the potential for long-term success in your career.

CHAPTER SIX

WHY PEOPLE BUY ANYTHING

Understanding the psychology behind why people buy is essential for anyone in sales, marketing, or business. It is not enough to simply know what your product is and how much it costs; you must understand why consumers make purchasing decisions in the first place. Why do people buy things they don't need? Why do they spend money on products or services that don't always offer a tangible return? The answers to these questions lie in the underlying emotions, desires, and psychological triggers that drive human behavior.

In this chapter, we will explore the core reasons why people buy anything, from basic needs to impulse purchases. By understanding these motivations, you can better position your product, refine your sales strategy, and build more successful, long-lasting relationships with your customers.

1. To Fulfill a Need or Solve a Problem

At the most fundamental level, people buy to solve a problem or fulfill a need. This need may be physical—like the need for food, shelter, or clothing—or emotional, such as the desire for security, status, or companionship. When a product or service is presented as the solution to a particular problem, it triggers the buyer's need for a resolution.

The Need for Problem-Solving: This is the simplest form of motivation, where the buyer identifies a gap in their life, and the purchase is the logical step to address that gap. This is why many businesses center their marketing around problem-solving—whether it's a cleaning product, a piece of software that streamlines work processes, or a car that provides a more efficient commute.

For example, a person buys an umbrella because it is raining, and they want to stay dry. The umbrella solves an immediate problem. In this case, the marketing might emphasize its practical benefits: "Stay dry, even in the heaviest downpours."

Key Insight: Understanding the problem your customer is trying to solve is the foundation for successful sales. When a product aligns with a clear need, the sale becomes almost inevitable.

2. To Improve Their Life or Enhance Their Experience

Humans are always looking for ways to improve their lives. Purchases are often driven by the desire for a better quality of life, more convenience, or a deeper sense of satisfaction. People buy things to make their lives easier, more enjoyable, or more comfortable. This goes beyond basic needs and taps into a more aspirational form of purchasing.

The Power of Aspiration: Products that promise to improve quality of life or enhance experiences tend to invoke emotional responses. For example, people might purchase a high-end coffee maker not because they need it, but because it will improve their daily routine and provide them with a more enjoyable, comforting experience. The idea of waking up to freshly brewed coffee can have a profound impact on someone's day.

Similarly, luxury items like high-end watches or designer handbags often aren't bought out of necessity but to fulfill a deeper emotional need—status, self-expression, or a sense of belonging to a certain social group.

Key Insight: The desire to improve one's life, whether through comfort, status, or personal enjoyment, is a powerful motivator. Buyers are often looking for products that promise to make their lives better or more fulfilling in some way.

3. To Feel a Sense of Belonging or Status

Humans are social creatures, and a significant part of why people buy things is to feel a sense of belonging, status, or validation. People make purchases to fit into a particular social group, to signal their status or identity, or to achieve a sense of exclusivity.

Social Proof and Status: Many purchasing decisions are influenced by social trends, peer pressure, and the need for approval from others. Think about high-end brands like Apple, Rolex, or Tesla. These products are often more expensive than their competitors, but people are willing to pay the premium because owning them confers a sense of belonging to a particular group or lifestyle.

Similarly, people may buy items that signal their status—whether it's a luxury car, designer clothing, or the latest tech gadget. These purchases are not always about the practical value of the item itself, but the message it sends to others about one's identity, success, or tastes.

Key Insight: People buy for social validation. Understanding the aspirational goals of your customers can help you tailor your marketing to appeal to their need for status or belonging.

4. To Avoid Pain or Loss

Another powerful motivator is the desire to avoid pain, discomfort, or loss. This is often seen in purchases that are driven by fear, urgency, or anxiety. Buyers may act impulsively when they perceive that not buying could result in a significant negative outcome.

The Fear of Missing Out (FOMO): Marketing strategies that capitalize on urgency or scarcity are incredibly effective because they tap into this fear of loss. Sales tactics like "limited-time offers" or "only a few left in stock" trigger the buyer's fear of missing out, leading them to make a purchase they might not have made otherwise. This fear-driven buying behavior is evident in industries like fashion, technology, and even real estate.

Similarly, people may buy insurance or health products because they want to avoid the pain of being unprepared for an unfortunate event or illness. This kind of purchasing is less about desire and more about preventing future loss or pain.

Key Insight: The fear of loss—whether it's missing an opportunity or failing to protect oneself from an adverse event—is a significant motivator. Buyers often act quickly when they believe in a potential negative outcome from not purchasing.

5. For Convenience or Time-Saving

In today's fast-paced world, people value convenience above almost anything else. The more time and effort a product saves, the more appealing it becomes. Purchases are often made because a product simplifies life, saves time, or makes a process more efficient.

The Value of Time: Take, for example, the rise of meal delivery services. People are buying these services not necessarily because they need food, but because it provides a convenient solution that saves time and effort. Similarly, subscription-based models—whether for streaming services, software, or household supplies—offer customers convenience by delivering value consistently with little to no effort on their part.

Time-saving products appeal to busy professionals, parents, and anyone looking to maximize their productivity or reduce their daily burdens. By positioning your product as a time-saver or efficiency booster, you can tap into one of the strongest motivations for modern consumers.

Key Insight: People buy to save time, simplify tasks, and make their lives easier. Positioning your product as a convenience solution can be a compelling sales tactic.

6. To Experience Enjoyment or Instant Gratification

People love pleasure. Whether it's an indulgence in a sweet treat, a spontaneous trip, or a new gadget that promises instant gratification, people are often motivated by the desire for pleasure or enjoyment. The ability to satisfy a desire quickly is a powerful driver of purchasing behavior.

Instant Gratification: In our modern world, instant gratification is more accessible than ever before. Online shopping, fast food, and digital entertainment allow people to satisfy their desires almost immediately. This has created a consumer environment where people are willing to spend on things that offer immediate satisfaction, even if they don't necessarily fulfill long-term needs.

Key Insight: People buy things that bring them immediate pleasure or satisfaction. By understanding the role of instant gratification in consumer behavior, businesses can tap into this desire with products that offer quick and tangible rewards.

Conclusion: Understanding the Core Motivations Behind Purchases

People buy for many reasons, but at the core, their decisions are driven by a complex mix of emotional and psychological factors. Whether it's fulfilling a need, improving their lives, gaining status, avoiding pain, saving time, or experiencing pleasure, understanding these motivations allows businesses and salespeople to connect more deeply with their customers.

The most successful sales strategies are those that align a product or service with the core motivations of the consumer. The more deeply you understand the "why" behind your customer's buying behavior, the more effectively you can communicate your value proposition and drive successful sales.

Ultimately, people buy because they believe it will benefit them in some way. By tapping into these fundamental human desires and motivations, you can unlock the keys to successful selling and build lasting relationships with your customers.

Here's a simple chart summarizing the key reasons why people buy anything, based on the motivations discussed in the chapter:

Motivation	Description	Examples	Sales Strategy
Fulfilling a Need or Solving a Problem	People buy to address a specific need or solve a problem.	- Buying food to curb hunger - Buying a washing machine to clean clothes	Focus on demonstrating how your product solves a specific problem or fulfills a need.
Improving Life or Enhancing Experience	Purchases that improve comfort, convenience, or quality of life.	- Buying a luxury car for comfort - Purchasing a coffee maker for better mornings	Highlight how your product enhances the buyer's daily life or improves their experiences.
Belonging or Status	Buying to fit in with a group, project a certain identity, or signal status.	- Luxury goods like Rolex or designer clothing - Social media products	Position your product as a status symbol or a means to fit into an aspirational group.
Avoiding Pain or Loss	Purchases made to avoid discomfort, loss, or a negative outcome.	- Health insurance - Purchasing an umbrella in a rainstorm	Use urgency, scarcity, or security benefits to create a fear of missing out or a fear of loss.
Convenience or Time-Saving	People buy to simplify tasks, save time, or make life more convenient.	- Meal delivery services - Subscription-based services like Netflix	Emphasize the time-saving and convenience benefits of your product or service.
Enjoyment or Instant Gratification	Purchases made to experience immediate pleasure or enjoyment.	- A fast food snack - Buying a new phone for its entertainment features	Market the immediate rewards and pleasures your product offers.

PART 2

POINTERS FOR STRESS MANAGEMENT WITH DEEP AND DISCIPLINED WORK

CHAPTER SEVEN

FROM STRESS TO SERINITY

In the 21ˢᵗ century, stress has become a universal companion. It affects almost everyone, whether it's from the pressures of work, family responsibilities, societal expectations, or personal goals. If not managed properly, stress can lead to physical, mental, and emotional exhaustion. In fact, it can sometimes feel like the harder we try to keep everything together, the more stress compounds. Yet, within this struggle, there lies a profound opportunity: the ability to transform stress into serenity—a state of inner calm, balance, and clarity, no matter what external circumstances may be.

This chapter explores the nature of stress, its effects, and practical strategies to reclaim serenity in your life. From recognizing the true cost of stress to incorporating mindfulness and self-compassion into your daily routine, we'll delve into how you can make the shift from a stressed-out existence to a peaceful, fulfilling one.

1. Understanding Stress: The Silent Overload

Stress isn't a modern phenomenon. Throughout history, humans have faced challenges and external threats that triggered the body's "fight or flight" response—an evolutionary mechanism designed to protect us from immediate danger. When faced with physical danger, the body reacts by releasing stress hormones like adrenaline and cortisol, which increase heart rate, prepare muscles for action, and focus the mind on immediate survival.

However, today's "threats" are often less immediate but more chronic—ranging from work deadlines and financial pressure to relationship issues and emotional overwhelm. This means that stress is no longer just a fleeting experience; it can build up over time, affecting the body and mind.

The Body's Response to Stress

When stress becomes chronic, it starts to affect the body in profound ways. The constant release of stress hormones can lead to a range of physical issues, including:

Increased heart rate and elevated blood pressure: Stress keeps the body in a heightened state of alertness, increasing the risk of cardiovascular diseases.

Weakened immune system: Prolonged stress suppresses the immune system, making it harder for the body to fight off infections and diseases.

Muscle tension: Chronic stress leads to tightness in the muscles, which can cause headaches, back pain, and even digestive issues.

Sleep disturbances: Stress affects sleep quality, leading to insomnia or restlessness, further exacerbating stress the next day.

Mentally, stress triggers anxiety, irritability, and feelings of being overwhelmed. Emotionally, it can lead to feelings of helplessness and burnout. If left unchecked, the stress response becomes a cycle—one that can be difficult to break without conscious intervention.

Story: Kajal'sWake-Up Call

Kajal, a senior executive in a multinational corporation, had always prided herself on her work ethic. Early in her career, she thrived under pressure, enjoying the excitement of fast-paced projects and the satisfaction of delivering results. However, over time, the demands of her job increased. Deadlines grew tighter, the expectations higher, and her personal time vanished into an endless list of tasks.

Despite her success, began to experience physical symptoms of stress—constant fatigue, a racing heart, and tension in her neck and shoulders. One day, while on a business trip, Kajal experienced a panic attack in the middle of a meeting. It was a wake-up call. She realized that what had once fueled her passion for her career was now draining her. Something had to change.

2. The Cost of Unchecked Stress

Unchecked stress does not only have a mental or emotional cost—it has a significant impact on physical health, relationships, and overall well-being. According to the American Psychological Association, prolonged exposure to stress can increase the risk of serious health conditions, such as:

Heart disease and stroke: Chronic stress can lead to cardiovascular problems, including high blood pressure, heart attacks, and strokes.

Mental health issues: Anxiety, depression, and burnout are commonly associated with chronic stress.

Digestive disorders: Stress has been linked to gastrointestinal issues such as irritable bowel syndrome (IBS) and acid reflux.

Chronic fatigue: The ongoing release of cortisol can cause long-term exhaustion, leaving individuals feeling drained and lacking energy.

Additionally, stress impacts personal relationships. When you're under constant pressure, it's easy to become irritable, withdrawn, or disengaged. You may snap at loved ones, find it hard to relax, or struggle with maintaining meaningful connections. Stress creates a barrier to truly enjoying life, both at work and at home.

Story: Siddarth's Wake-Up Call

Siddarth, a successful father of two, was living a life that many would envy. A high-paying job in a finance firm, a beautiful home, and a loving family—on the surface, everything seemed perfect. Yet, Siddarth's life was consumed by stress. He constantly worked long hours, sacrificed sleep, and neglected his health. The pressure from work piled on, and at home, he found himself often grumpy and impatient.

One night, after a heated argument with his wife over something trivial,Siddarth realized how badly his stress was affecting his personal life. He had grown distant from his family, disconnected from his friends, and his health was deteriorating. It was in that moment of frustration and guilt that Siddarth understood: he needed to change the way he approached life.

3. The Path to Serenity: Shifting Your Mindset

The first step in moving from stress to serenity is a fundamental shift in how we view stress itself. Rather than seeing stress as something to be eliminated or avoided, we can begin to see it as an experience to be managed. By shifting our mindset, we can transform how we respond to stress, leading to greater resilience, peace, and clarity.

a) Mindfulness: Awareness in the Present Moment

One of the most effective ways to manage stress and cultivate serenity is through mindfulness. Mindfulness involves bringing your full attention to the present moment, without judgment or distraction. It allows you to observe your thoughts, emotions, and bodily sensations in real time, without getting caught up in them.

By practicing mindfulness, we begin to recognize the signs of stress before they become overwhelming. Instead of reacting automatically to stress, mindfulness helps you respond more thoughtfully.

Practical Tip: Practice mindful breathing for five minutes every morning. Sit in a comfortable position, close your eyes, and focus on the sensation of your breath as it enters and exits your body. When your mind starts to wander (and it will), gently guide your attention back to your breath.

Story: Sophia's Transformation

Sophia, a nurse working in a busy hospital, struggled with stress due to the fast-paced environment. She often felt overwhelmed by the constant influx of patients, the long shifts, and the emotional toll of her work. One day, after a particularly challenging day, Sophia decided to try something new—mindfulness. She started taking small breaks during her shifts to focus on her breath and regain a sense of calm. Gradually, she found herself less reactive to stress, more focused, and able to approach challenges with greater clarity. This practice of mindfulness transformed how she experienced stress, bringing serenity even during the busiest days.

b) Self-Compassion: Treating Yourself with Kindness

Self-compassion is the practice of treating yourself with the same kindness, care, and understanding that you would offer a dear friend. When we are under stress, we often criticize ourselves harshly, thinking we need to be perfect or do everything on our own. Self-compassion, however, encourages self-acceptance, allowing us to face difficulties with patience and understanding.

Practical Tip: Start each day by acknowledging something you appreciate about yourself. It could be a simple achievement or a quality you admire in yourself. Over time, this practice will help you treat yourself with kindness, especially during stressful times.

Story: Aniket's Awakening

Aniket was a small business owner who prided himself on being a perfectionist. He pushed himself to the limit, often staying late into the night to ensure everything was running smoothly. However, this drive to be perfect led him to ignore his personal needs, and his stress levels skyrocketed. One day, Aniket made a decision: he would treat himself with the same compassion he showed his employees and family. Instead of berating himself for mistakes, he began to practice self-compassion, acknowledging his efforts and allowing himself time to recharge. Over time, this shift brought greater serenity into his work and life.

c) Gratitude: Shifting Focus from What's Wrong to What's Right

Gratitude is a powerful antidote to stress. When we focus on what's going wrong, it only fuels our feelings of frustration and helplessness. However, when we practice gratitude, we shift our attention to what's going right in our lives. This shift in perspective helps us appreciate the present moment and see the beauty, even in the midst of challenges.

Practical Tip: Start a gratitude journal. Each day, write down three things you are grateful for, no matter how small. This simple practice can help reframe your perspective and bring a sense of calm and serenity.

Story: Rani's Gratitude Journey

Rani, a busy mother of three, felt overwhelmed by the demands of her life. Between managing her family, career, and household responsibilities, she felt like she was constantly running on empty. One evening, feeling especially exhausted,Rani decided to try something different: she started a gratitude journal. Each night, before bed, she listed three things she was grateful for. Over time, Rani noticed a profound shift in her perspective. She began to focus on the positive aspects of her life—her children's laughter, her supportive partner, the simple joys of life. Gratitude became her anchor, and with it, serenity followed.

4. Creating Practical Rituals for Serenity

While mindset shifts are essential, it's also important to establish practical rituals that help you manage stress and maintain serenity. These rituals become anchors—tools you can rely on to return to a place of peace when life gets overwhelming.

Morning Routine: Starting your day with intention can set the tone for the rest of the day. Incorporate rituals like meditation, yoga, or journaling to center yourself before the day's demands.

Physical Activity: Exercise releases endorphins, which are natural stress relievers. Even a short walk can help clear your mind and reduce tension.

Digital Detox: Unplugging from screens can help you reconnect with yourself and reduce feelings of overwhelm.

Conclusion: From Stress to Serenity

The transition from stress to serenity is not a one-time event, but a continuous journey. It requires conscious effort, patience, and a willingness to practice self-awareness, self-compassion, and gratitude. By shifting your mindset and incorporating practical tools, you can begin to transform stress from a source of overwhelm into a source of growth and resilience.

As you navigate the complexities of life, remember that serenity is not the absence of stress—it is the ability to find peace within it. Through small, consistent practices, you can create a life that is not only more peaceful, but also more fulfilling.

A detailed chart that visually represents the key aspects of the journey from stress to serenity, outlining strategies and practices to help manage stress and foster inner calm.

Key Aspect	Stress	Path to Serenity	Practical Strategies
Understanding Stress	Fight-or-flight response triggered by external stressors (work, family, finances)	Acknowledging that stress is a natural part of life, but that it can be managed	Self-awareness, mindfulness, understanding stress triggers
Physical Impact	Increased heart rate, elevated blood pressure, fatigue, muscle tension	Restoring balance through relaxation and self-care	Mindful breathing, relaxation techniques, sleep hygiene
Mental Impact	Anxiety, irritability, overwhelm, fatigue	Shifting perspective to respond thoughtfully to stress	Mindfulness, reframing negative thoughts, self-compassion
Emotional Impact	Frustration, anger, helplessness	Developing emotional resilience and acceptance	Gratitude practice, emotional awareness, self-compassion
Mindset Shift	Reactionary and automatic response to stress	Conscious choice to embrace serenity and manage stress	Mindfulness, meditation, stress management practices

Mindfulness & Presence	Distracted, unable to focus on the present moment	Deep focus on the present moment without judgment	Daily meditation, mindful breathing, journaling
Self-Compassion	Self-criticism, guilt for perceived shortcomings	Kindness towards oneself, treating yourself with care	Positive affirmations, treating yourself like a friend
Gratitude	Focusing on what's wrong, negativity	Shifting focus to what's right and appreciating life's positives	Daily gratitude journaling, expressing thanks, focusing on positives
Daily Rituals for Calm	Chaotic routines, no time for self-care	Consistent rituals that promote inner peace and balance	Morning routine, physical activity, digital detox
Physical Health	Increased susceptibility to illness due to weakened immune system	Restoring physical health through stress reduction techniques	Exercise, proper nutrition, hydration, relaxation

Summary:

- Stress is a natural, physical response to external challenges but can have long-term negative effects on our health and well-being if left unchecked.
- The Path to Serenity requires a mindset shift that focuses on self-awareness, mindfulness, self-compassion, and gratitude.
- Practical Strategies such as mindful breathing, exercise, gratitude journaling, and relaxation techniques help to mitigate the effects of stress and create a more peaceful, balanced life.

CHAPTER EIGHT

DEEP WORK – THE PATH TO UNPARALLELED FOCUS AND SUCCESS

Introduction

In an age of constant distractions and information overload, the ability to focus deeply has become an exceptional and highly valuable skill. Deep Work, a term popularized by Cal Newport, refers to the practice of focusing on cognitively demanding tasks without distractions. This focused state not only allows for high-quality work but also cultivates a sense of accomplishment and mastery. This chapter delves into the philosophy, practices, and stories that underline the transformative power of deep work.

Section 1: Understanding Deep Work

Deep work is characterized by:

1. Intense Focus: Working on a single task with full attention.

2. Complexity: Tackling challenges that require significant mental effort.

3. Flow State: Entering a zone where time seems to disappear, and productivity skyrockets.

In contrast, shallow work includes tasks like answering emails, attending non-essential meetings, or scrolling through social media. While shallow work is unavoidable, prioritizing deep work is what separates the truly exceptional from the average.

The Science Behind Focus

Research in neuroscience shows that deep work taps into a brain state called flow. When in flow, the brain produces gamma waves associated with peak performance and creativity. Moreover, sustained focus strengthens neural connections, making subsequent deep work easier.

Case Study: Carl Friedrich Gauss

The legendary mathematician Carl Friedrich Gauss exemplified deep work. Known for his groundbreaking discoveries in mathematics, Gauss would isolate himself from distractions for hours. His ability to concentrate intensely enabled him to develop theories that are still studied today. His work ethic demonstrates the power of a focused mind.

Section 2: Why Deep Work Matters in the Modern World

Today, the value of deep work has risen due to:

Economic Shifts: Jobs increasingly demand creative problem-solving and high-level expertise.

Digital Distractions: Constant notifications and multitasking erode focus and productivity.

Competitive Advantage: Those who cultivate deep work produce exceptional results and gain an edge.

Story: J.K. Rowling and the Final Harry Potter Book

While writing Harry Potter and the Deathly Hallows, J.K. Rowling checked into the Balmoral Hotel in Edinburgh to isolate herself from distractions. In this focused environment, she completed one of the most awaited books of the decade. Her decision to prioritize deep work over daily demands underscores its importance in producing exceptional work.

Section 3: The Challenges of Deep Work

Deep work is not easy. The modern world bombards us with:

1. Distractions: Social media, emails, and interruptions.

2. Cognitive Resistance: The brain naturally seeks easier, less demanding activities.

3. Cultural Misalignment: Many workplaces value being "busy" over producing meaningful results.
    Personal Story: Overcoming Distractions
A young entrepreneur, Ravi, struggled to write his first book amidst daily interruptions. Determined to overcome this, he created a "deep work ritual": waking up at 5 a.m., locking his phone in another room, and writing for three hours. This disciplined approach transformed his productivity, allowing him to finish his manuscript within six months.

Section 4: Cultivating Deep Work – Practices and Strategies

1. Time Blocking
Allocate specific blocks of time for deep work. Treat these as non-negotiable appointments with yourself.
    2. Create a Ritual
Develop a pre-work routine to signal your brain that it's

time to focus. This could include meditation, journaling, or listening to specific music.

3. Optimize Your Environment

Minimize distractions by:

Using noise-canceling headphones.

Working in a clean, uncluttered space.

Setting boundaries with family or colleagues.

4. Digital Minimalism

Reduce the number of apps, notifications, and platforms you use. Tools like Freedom or Forest can help block distractions.

5. Embrace Monotony

Train your brain to be comfortable with boredom by avoiding constant stimulation. For example, take a walk without your phone or avoid multitasking.

6. End-of-Day Shutdown

Create a ritual to end your workday. This could involve reviewing accomplishments, setting priorities for tomorrow, and switching off mentally.

Story: Bill Gates' "Think Weeks"

Bill Gates famously takes "think weeks" twice a year, retreating to a cabin with no internet or distractions. These weeks have been critical in shaping Microsoft's strategy and Gates' philanthropic vision.

Section 5: The Long-Term Benefits of Deep Work

Practicing deep work has profound effects on both professional and personal life:

Skill Mastery: Deep work accelerates the learning of complex skills.

Career Growth: Producing exceptional work leads to recognition and opportunities.

Emotional Fulfillment: Entering flow states enhances happiness and reduces stress.

Legacy Building: Deep work enables the creation of work that endures.

Historical Example: Nikola Tesla
Tesla's ability to work deeply allowed him to conceptualize and develop groundbreaking inventions like alternating current and wireless communication. His legacy is a testament to the enduring impact of focused, high-quality work.

Section 6: Overcoming Resistance to Deep Work

When starting deep work, you may face:
Mental Fatigue: Your brain will resist initial efforts.
Impatience: Results take time to manifest.

Solution: Start small. Dedicate 30 minutes daily to deep work and gradually increase the duration. Reward yourself for progress to reinforce the habit.

Conclusion

Deep work is not merely a productivity strategy; it is a path to mastery, fulfillment, and success. In a world that constantly pulls us toward shallow distractions, committing to deep work is a radical act of self-respect and ambition. By cultivating this skill, you can unlock your full potential and create work that stands the test of time.

"To produce at your peak level, you need to work for extended periods with full concentration. Deep work is the key to your ultimate productivity." – Cal Newport

Introduction

In an age of constant distractions and information overload, the ability to focus deeply has become an exceptional and highly valuable skill. Deep Work, a term popularized by Cal Newport, refers to the practice of focusing on cognitively demanding tasks without distractions. This focused state not only allows for high-quality work but also cultivates a sense of accomplishment and mastery. This chapter delves into the philosophy, practices, and stories that underline the transformative power of deep work.

Section 1: Understanding Deep Work

Deep work is characterized by:

1. Intense Focus: Working on a single task with full attention.

2. Complexity: Tackling challenges that require significant mental effort.

3. Flow State: Entering a zone where time seems to disappear, and productivity skyrockets.

In contrast, shallow work includes tasks like answering emails, attending non-essential meetings, or scrolling through social media. While shallow work is unavoidable, prioritizing deep work is what separates the truly exceptional from the average.

The Science Behind Focus

Research in neuroscience shows that deep work taps into a brain state called flow. When in flow, the brain produces gamma waves associated with peak performance and creativity. Moreover, sustained focus strengthens neural connections, making subsequent deep work easier.

Case Study: Carl Friedrich Gauss

The legendary mathematician Carl Friedrich Gauss exemplified deep work. Known for his groundbreaking discoveries in mathematics, Gauss would isolate himself from distractions for hours. His ability to concentrate intensely enabled him to develop theories that are still studied today. His work ethic demonstrates the power of a focused mind.

Section 2: Why Deep Work Matters in the Modern World

Today, the value of deep work has risen due to:

Economic Shifts: Jobs increasingly demand creative problem-solving and high-level expertise.

Digital Distractions: Constant notifications and multitasking erode focus and productivity.

Competitive Advantage: Those who cultivate deep work produce exceptional results and gain an edge.

Story: J.K. Rowling and the Final Harry Potter Book
While writing Harry Potter and the Deathly Hallows, J.K. Rowling checked into the Balmoral Hotel in Edinburgh to isolate herself from distractions. In this focused

environment, she completed one of the most awaited books of the decade. Her decision to prioritize deep work over daily demands underscores its importance in producing exceptional work.

Section 3: The Challenges of Deep Work

Deep work is not easy. The modern world bombards us with:

1. Distractions: Social media, emails, and interruptions.

2. Cognitive Resistance: The brain naturally seeks easier, less demanding activities.

3. Cultural Misalignment: Many workplaces value being "busy" over producing meaningful results.

Personal Story: Overcoming Distractions

A young entrepreneur, Ravi, struggled to write his first book amidst daily interruptions. Determined to overcome this, he created a "deep work ritual": waking up at 5 a.m., locking his phone in another room, and writing for three hours. This disciplined approach transformed his productivity, allowing him to finish his manuscript within six months.

Section 4: Cultivating Deep Work – Practices and Strategies

1. Time Blocking

Allocate specific blocks of time for deep work. Treat these as non-negotiable appointments with yourself.

2. Create a Ritual

Develop a pre-work routine to signal your brain that it's

time to focus. This could include meditation, journaling, or listening to specific music.

3. Optimize Your Environment

Minimize distractions by:

Using noise-canceling headphones.

Working in a clean, uncluttered space.

Setting boundaries with family or colleagues.

4. Digital Minimalism

Reduce the number of apps, notifications, and platforms you use. Tools like Freedom or Forest can help block distractions.

5. Embrace Monotony

Train your brain to be comfortable with boredom by avoiding constant stimulation. For example, take a walk without your phone or avoid multitasking.

6. End-of-Day Shutdown

Create a ritual to end your workday. This could involve reviewing accomplishments, setting priorities for tomorrow, and switching off mentally.

Story: Bill Gates' "Think Weeks"

Bill Gates famously takes "think weeks" twice a year, retreating to a cabin with no internet or distractions. These weeks have been critical in shaping Microsoft's strategy and Gates' philanthropic vision.

Section 5: The Long-Term Benefits of Deep Work

Practicing deep work has profound effects on both professional and personal life:

Skill Mastery: Deep work accelerates the learning of complex skills.

Career Growth: Producing exceptional work leads to recognition and opportunities.

Emotional Fulfillment: Entering flow states enhances happiness and reduces stress.

Legacy Building: Deep work enables the creation of work that endures.

Historical Example: Nikola Tesla
Tesla's ability to work deeply allowed him to conceptualize and develop groundbreaking inventions like alternating current and wireless communication. His legacy is a testament to the enduring impact of focused, high-quality work.

Section 6: Overcoming Resistance to Deep Work
When starting deep work, you may face:
Mental Fatigue: Your brain will resist initial efforts.
Impatience: Results take time to manifest.

Solution: Start small. Dedicate 30 minutes daily to deep work and gradually increase the duration. Reward yourself for progress to reinforce the habit.

Conclusion
Deep work is not merely a productivity strategy; it is a path to mastery, fulfillment, and success. In a world that constantly pulls us toward shallow distractions, committing to deep work is a radical act of self-respect and ambition. By cultivating this skill, you can unlock your full potential and create work that stands the test of time.

"To produce at your peak level, you need to work for extended periods with full concentration. Deep work is the key to your ultimate productivity." – Cal Newport

CHAPTER NINE

SELF-DISCIPLINE – THE FOUNDATION OF LASTING SUCCESS

Introduction

Self-discipline is the cornerstone of personal growth and achievement. It is the ability to control impulses, delay gratification, and remain committed to long-term goals despite challenges. Unlike motivation, which is fleeting, self-discipline creates a steady path to success. This chapter explores the essence of self-discipline, its benefits, strategies for cultivating it, and stories of individuals who mastered it to achieve greatness.

Section 1: What is Self-Discipline?

Self-discipline is the practice of making decisions and taking actions that align with your goals, even when it's difficult or inconvenient. It involves:

1. Self-Control: Resisting temptations that divert attention from your objectives.

2. Consistency: Showing up every day, regardless of how you feel.

3. Resilience: Pushing through discomfort and setbacks.
   Example: Serena Williams' Routine
Serena Williams, one of the greatest tennis players of all time, exemplifies self-discipline. Her rigorous training schedule, strict diet, and unwavering focus on improvement allowed her to dominate the sport for decades. Even during personal and physical challenges, she consistently showed up and worked harder than her competition.

Section 2: Why is Self-Discipline Important?

1. Achieving Goals: It bridges the gap between dreams and reality.

2. Building Confidence: Accomplishing small tasks consistently boosts self-belief.

3. Resisting Instant Gratification: It helps you prioritize long-term rewards over fleeting pleasures.

4. Enhancing Decision-Making: Self-disciplined people make rational, goal-oriented choices.

Story: The Marshmallow Experiment
In the 1970s, psychologist Walter Mischel conducted an experiment where children were given a choice: eat one marshmallow immediately or wait 15 minutes and get two. Those who resisted temptation and waited were found to have better life outcomes, including higher academic achievements and better emotional control. This study underscores the long-term benefits of self-discipline.

Section 3: The Challenges of Self-Discipline

Self-discipline is often undermined by:
Procrastination: Delaying tasks leads to missed opportunities.
Distractions: Social media, entertainment, and external noise.
Emotional Turmoil: Stress and emotional exhaustion drain willpower.
Lack of Clarity: Unclear goals reduce the motivation to stay disciplined.

Personal Story: Ramesh's Journey to Fitness
Ramesh, a corporate employee, struggled with obesity for years. Despite initial enthusiasm, he often gave up on diets and exercise routines. One day, he decided to start small—walking 10 minutes daily. Over months, his discipline grew. He gradually incorporated strength training and healthy eating, ultimately losing 30 kilograms.

His journey highlights that self-discipline grows with consistent, small actions.

Section 4: Strategies to Cultivate Self-Discipline

1. Set Clear Goals
Define your objectives clearly. Ambiguity breeds inaction. Use the SMART framework: Specific, Measurable, Achievable, Relevant, Time-bound.
2. Build Habits
Discipline becomes easier when your actions are habitual. For example, brushing your teeth requires no willpower because it's ingrained. Similarly, establish habits for important tasks.
3. Prioritize Tasks
Focus on high-impact activities. Use tools like the Eisenhower Matrix to separate urgent from important tasks.
4. Practice Delayed Gratification
Train yourself to resist immediate temptations by visualizing long-term rewards.
5. Create a Routine
A structured daily routine minimizes decision fatigue. For instance, Mark Zuckerberg's habit of wearing similar outfits eliminates trivial decisions, allowing more energy for meaningful work.
6. Accountability Partners
Share your goals with someone who can hold you accountable. Knowing someone is watching often enhances discipline.

7. Reward Yourself

Reinforce self-discipline by celebrating milestones. Rewards create positive associations with disciplined behavior.

Example: Benjamin Franklin's Journals

Benjamin Franklin tracked his habits daily, rating himself on virtues like temperance, industry, and humility. His meticulous journaling kept him accountable and allowed him to refine his behavior over time.

Section 5: Self-Discipline in Action

Story: The Transformation of Arnold Schwarzenegger

Arnold Schwarzenegger's journey from an Austrian farm boy to a global icon in bodybuilding, Hollywood, and politics is a testament to self-discipline. He followed an intense training regimen, waking up before dawn to lift weights. Even as a struggling actor, he maintained a rigorous schedule, honing his craft and learning English. His discipline laid the foundation for his unparalleled success in multiple fields.

Historical Example: Mahatma Gandhi

Mahatma Gandhi's disciplined life was rooted in simplicity and self-restraint. He adhered to strict principles, including fasting, meditation, and non-violence, even under extreme adversity. His disciplined approach inspired millions and played a crucial role in India's independence.

Section 6: Overcoming Setbacks

Even disciplined individuals face setbacks. What matters is how you recover.

Reframe Failures: View setbacks as learning opportunities.

Practice Forgiveness: Don't let guilt derail progress. Accept mistakes and move forward.

Reassess Goals: Ensure your goals are realistic and aligned with your values.

Story: Elon Musk's Perseverance
When SpaceX faced multiple rocket failures, Elon Musk could have given up. Instead, he stayed disciplined, refining designs and rallying his team. His persistence led to SpaceX becoming a pioneer in space exploration. Musk's journey demonstrates that discipline includes perseverance through failure.

Section 7: The Long-Term Benefits of Self-Discipline

1. Success in All Areas: Self-discipline impacts career, health, relationships, and personal development.

2. Resilience: Disciplined people handle stress and challenges better.

3. Personal Fulfillment: Living a disciplined life fosters a sense of control and purpose.

4. Legacy Creation: Discipline enables you to create work that endures.

Example: Thomas Edison's Tenacity

Edison famously said, "I have not failed. I've just found 10,000 ways that won't work." His disciplined approach to experimentation led to the invention of the light bulb, revolutionizing the world.

Conclusion

Self-discipline is the key to unlocking your potential. While the journey may be challenging, its rewards are profound. By mastering self-discipline, you gain control over your actions, overcome obstacles, and move closer to your dreams. Remember, discipline isn't a trait you're born with—it's a skill you cultivate daily through consistent effort.

"Discipline is the bridge between goals and accomplishment." – Jim Rohn

CHAPTER TEN

BRAHMACHARYA – THE PATH OF SELF-MASTERY AND SPIRITUAL GROWTH

Introduction

Brahmacharya, one of the core principles in ancient Indian philosophy, is often translated as "self-restraint" or "control over senses." Rooted in the Sanskrit words Brahman (the ultimate reality) and Acharya (practice or conduct), Brahmacharya emphasizes living a disciplined life dedicated to spiritual growth and higher consciousness. Although commonly associated with celibacy, its essence extends far beyond to include mastery over desires, focus on self-realization, and harmonious living.

This chapter explores the profound meaning of Brahmacharya, its role in personal transformation, practical application in modern life, and stories of individuals who exemplified its principles.

Section 1: Understanding Brahmacharya

In traditional Indian philosophy, Brahmacharya is one of the Yamas (ethical principles) in Patanjali's Yoga Sutras. It signifies:

1. Control Over Senses: Regulating sensory indulgence to prevent distraction from life's higher purpose.

2. Focus on Higher Goals: Channeling physical, mental, and emotional energy toward self-realization.

3. Balance and Moderation: Practicing restraint in all areas of life, not just sexuality.

Brahmacharya doesn't imply suppression but transformation—redirecting energy from material pursuits to spiritual growth.

Example: The Lamp and Oil Analogy

Just as a lamp's flame grows brighter when its oil is conserved, human potential shines when physical and mental energy are preserved and directed meaningfully.

Section 2: The Historical Significance of Brahmacharya

In ancient India, life was divided into four ashramas (stages):

1. Brahmacharya (Student Stage): A phase of disciplined learning and self-control.

2. Grihastha (Householder Stage): Engaging in family and societal responsibilities.

3. Vanaprastha (Retirement Stage): Gradual withdrawal from worldly life.

4. Sannyasa (Renunciation Stage): Complete focus on spiritual liberation.

Brahmacharya, as the foundation of life, prepared individuals for the responsibilities and challenges of subsequent stages.

Story: Swami Vivekananda's Brahmacharya
Swami Vivekananda attributed his intellectual brilliance, boundless energy, and spiritual power to Brahmacharya. By practicing self-restraint, he conserved his vital energy, enabling him to inspire millions worldwide and establish the Ramakrishna Mission.

Section 3: The Core Benefits of Brahmacharya

1. Mental Clarity
Restraint in sensory indulgence prevents mental

turbulence, allowing for clear and focused thought.

2. Physical Vitality
Conservation of energy through moderation enhances physical health and vitality.

3. Spiritual Growth
By transcending desires, individuals connect deeply with their inner selves and the divine.

4. Improved Relationships
Self-restraint fosters emotional stability and prevents conflicts caused by unchecked desires.

Example: Mahatma Gandhi's Practice of Brahmacharya Mahatma Gandhi adopted Brahmacharya not only as celibacy but as a way to purify his thoughts, speech, and actions. He believed this discipline amplified his moral strength and leadership ability, helping him guide India's struggle for independence.

Section 4: Practical Application of Brahmacharya in Modern Life

1. Mindful Consumption
Control over the mind begins with regulating what you consume—whether it's food, media, or information. Avoid overindulgence and seek balance.

2. Focus on Purpose
Identify higher goals in life. Redirect energy wasted on distractions toward achieving meaningful aspirations.

3. Meditation and Yoga
These practices calm the mind and enhance self-awareness, making it easier to practice restraint.

4. Healthy Boundaries
Limit exposure to environments or habits that trigger temptations.

5. Time Management
Discipline in managing time ensures energy is allocated to productive and uplifting activities.
Story: A Modern Professional's Journey
An IT professional, Priya, found herself overwhelmed by excessive work, social media, and late-night indulgences. Inspired by Brahmacharya, she started practicing digital detox, adopted a regular meditation routine, and focused on her long-term career goals. Over time, her productivity soared, and her stress levels dropped, demonstrating the relevance of Brahmacharya in contemporary life.

Section 5: Overcoming Challenges in Practicing Brahmacharya

Practicing Brahmacharya is challenging, especially in a world of constant stimulation and instant gratification.
Challenge 1: Overcoming Desires
Solution: Shift focus from suppression to redirection. Replace harmful habits with constructive ones like reading or exercising.

Challenge 2: Social Pressures
Solution: Stay committed to your values and find a supportive community that respects your choices.
Challenge 3: Maintaining Consistency
Solution: Develop small, sustainable practices and track progress through journaling or habit trackers.

Story: Buddha's Enlightenment
Before attaining enlightenment, Siddhartha Gautama (Buddha) practiced extreme asceticism, nearly starving himself. Realizing the futility of such extremes, he adopted the Middle Way—a balanced approach of moderation and self-discipline. This realization paved the way for his spiritual awakening and teachings.

Section 6: The Essence of Brahmacharya in Everyday Life

Brahmacharya is not limited to monks or spiritual seekers. Its principles can enhance daily life:

1. In Relationships: Practice emotional restraint and respect boundaries to build meaningful connections.

2. In Work: Channel focus into tasks without succumbing to procrastination or distractions.

3. In Health: Avoid overindulgence in food, alcohol, or other pleasures that harm the body.
    Example: Steve Jobs' Simplicity
Steve Jobs embodied aspects of Brahmacharya through his minimalist lifestyle. By avoiding distractions and focusing

his energy, he was able to channel creativity into revolutionary products like the iPhone and MacBook.

Section 7: The Ultimate Goal of Brahmacharya

The ultimate purpose of Brahmacharya is to:
   1. Transcend Desires: Move beyond material cravings to achieve inner peace.

2. Realize the Self: Attain self-mastery and connect with the higher self or divine consciousness.

3. Live Harmoniously: Cultivate a life of balance, free from excess and turmoil.
   Quote from Bhagavad Gita (6.5)
"One must elevate oneself by one's own mind and not degrade oneself. The mind is the friend of the conditioned soul, and it is also the enemy."

Conclusion

Brahmacharya is more than abstinence; it is a way of life rooted in self-mastery, balance, and spiritual growth. It offers a timeless framework to conserve energy, focus on higher goals, and lead a fulfilling life. In a world often driven by excess, Brahmacharya serves as a guiding light, helping us navigate toward inner peace and ultimate truth.

"By practicing Brahmacharya, the door to higher wisdom opens." – Swami Sivananda

CHAPTER ELEVEN

THE ART OF TINY TWEAKS

In a world that often celebrates dramatic transformations, the power of incremental improvement—what we call "tiny tweaks"—is frequently overlooked. Yet, history, science, and personal anecdotes affirm that small, consistent changes can lead to monumental outcomes over time. Mastering the art of tiny tweaks is about leveraging the compounding power of progress to achieve growth, resilience, and fulfillment.

What Are Tiny Tweaks?

Tiny tweaks are minor adjustments to behaviors, habits, or routines that, while seemingly insignificant in isolation, accumulate into meaningful change. They are the antithesis of sweeping overhauls, focusing instead on attainable shifts that are easy to implement and sustain. For instance:

In health: Choosing stairs over elevators.

In productivity: Starting the day by planning three key tasks.

In relationships: Spending five extra minutes listening attentively to loved ones.

These adjustments are non-disruptive but impactful over time.

Why Tiny Tweaks Work

Psychological Accessibility:

Large goals can feel overwhelming, leading to procrastination or burnout. Tiny tweaks, on the other hand, are manageable, reducing resistance to change and fostering a sense of accomplishment.

Momentum Creation:

Progress, no matter how small, creates momentum. Achieving one tweak inspires further action, creating a cycle of motivation and achievement.

The Power of Compounding:

Like financial interest, small improvements compound over time. A 1% daily improvement may feel trivial, but it results in exponential growth when sustained.

Sustainability:

Radical changes are often short-lived due to their disruptive nature. Tiny tweaks fit seamlessly into daily routines, making them easier to maintain.

Areas Where Tiny Tweaks Shine

Personal Growth:

Small adjustments to daily habits, like reading a page of a book each day or meditating for two minutes, can accumulate into profound self-improvement.

Professional Success:

Incremental skill development, like learning a new term in a foreign language daily, leads to mastery without overwhelming effort.

Health and Wellness:

Replacing soda with water or adding an extra five minutes of movement each day can significantly improve long-term health.

Relationships:

A simple practice like expressing gratitude daily

strengthens bonds and fosters emotional connections.

How to Embrace the Art of Tiny Tweaks

Start Small:
Identify a single aspect of your life you'd like to improve. Define the smallest actionable step to address it.
   Be Consistent:
Consistency is the backbone of tiny tweaks. Regular practice transforms small changes into ingrained habits.
   Celebrate Wins:
Acknowledge and celebrate even minor progress. Positive reinforcement sustains motivation.
   Reassess and Refine:
Periodically evaluate the impact of your tweaks. Adjust or add new tweaks to align with evolving goals.
   Leverage Feedback:
Seek input from others or track metrics to understand the effectiveness of your tweaks. This ensures you stay on the path to improvement.

Real-Life Examples of Tiny Tweaks

James Clear's 1% Rule:

In Atomic Habits, Clear emphasizes that improving by just 1% each day can lead to remarkable transformation over time. This principle illustrates the compounding power of tiny changes.

Kaizen in Business:

The Japanese philosophy of Kaizen—continuous improvement through small changes—has revolutionized industries worldwide, proving that incremental progress drives sustainable success.

Personal Triumphs:

Stories abound of individuals who turned their lives around by making one small adjustment at a time, whether it was taking a daily walk, writing one paragraph a day, or committing to a gratitude practice.

The Ripple Effect of Tiny Tweaks

Tiny tweaks not only impact the individual but also extend their influence outward. A small change in your attitude or actions can inspire others, improve your environment, and shift outcomes in unforeseen ways.

By focusing on the art of tiny tweaks, you align yourself with a philosophy of growth that is accessible, adaptable, and profoundly effective. Whether the goal is to lead a healthier life, build meaningful relationships, or achieve professional success, tiny tweaks offer a path that is both realistic and transformative.

The journey of a thousand miles, as the saying goes, begins with a single step—and perhaps, a tiny tweak.

5 Stories Based On Real Life Incident From Which We Can Learn

1. Oprah Winfrey: From Poverty to Media Mogul

Born in 1954 in rural Mississippi, Oprah Winfrey grew up in extreme poverty. She lived with her grandmother, who taught her to read before the age of three. Her early years were marked by abuse and instability as she moved between her parents' homes.

Despite these hardships, Oprah excelled in school. She won a full scholarship to Tennessee State University and began working in local media. At 19, she became the youngest and first African-American woman news anchor at a local station.

Her big break came when she was offered the opportunity to host a struggling talk show, AM Chicago. Oprah transformed the show into a massive success by focusing on personal stories and empathetic interviews, eventually rebranding it as The Oprah Winfrey Show. The show dominated daytime television for 25 years, making her the richest African-American woman in history.

Oprah used her platform to advocate for education and philanthropy. She opened the Oprah Winfrey Leadership Academy for Girls in South Africa and donated millions to charitable causes.

Lesson: Resilience, education, and empathy can overcome even the harshest of beginnings.

2. Abraham Lincoln: The Self-Taught President

Abraham Lincoln was born in a one-room log cabin in 1809, in the frontier of Kentucky. His family was poor, and formal schooling was sparse, amounting to less than a year in total. Lincoln taught himself to read and write using borrowed books, often walking miles to access them.

As a young man, Lincoln worked odd jobs, including splitting logs and running a store. His interest in law led him to borrow legal books and study independently. He passed the bar exam and became a self-taught lawyer, earning respect for his logical reasoning and eloquence.

Lincoln's political career began in the Illinois state legislature, and he later served a term in Congress. His opposition to the expansion of slavery set him apart, but he faced repeated electoral defeats before becoming the 16th President of the United States in 1861.

As president, Lincoln faced the monumental challenge of leading a divided nation through the Civil War. His leadership preserved the Union and ended slavery through the Emancipation Proclamation and the passage of the 13th Amendment. Tragically, he was assassinated in 1865, but his legacy as one of America's greatest leaders endures.

Lesson: Perseverance, self-education, and moral conviction can lead to transformative leadership.

3. Marie Curie: A Legacy of Dedication and Discovery

Marie Curie, born in 1867 in Warsaw, Poland, was a trailblazer in science. As a young woman, she faced gender discrimination that barred her from attending university in Poland. Undeterred, she moved to Paris to study at the Sorbonne, working tirelessly to master physics and mathematics.

Curie married Pierre Curie, a fellow scientist, and the two collaborated on groundbreaking research. They discovered the elements polonium and radium, which earned them a Nobel Prize in Physics in 1903, making Marie the first woman to receive the prestigious award.

After Pierre's untimely death in 1906, Marie continued their work, later winning a second Nobel Prize in Chemistry in 1911 for her isolation of radium and studies of radioactivity. Her discoveries paved the way for X-ray technology and cancer treatments.

Despite her achievements, Curie faced significant challenges, including financial struggles, health problems caused by radiation exposure, and sexism within the scientific community. Yet, her determination never wavered.

Lesson: Passion, hard work, and resilience can shatter barriers and change the world.

4. Stephen Hawking: Triumph Over Disability

Stephen Hawking was born in 1942 in Oxford, England. A bright student with a love for mathematics and physics, he enrolled at the University of Cambridge for postgraduate studies.

At 21, Hawking was diagnosed with amyotrophic lateral sclerosis (ALS), a degenerative motor neuron disease. Doctors gave him just two years to live. Initially devastated, he found new purpose in his studies and relationships.

Despite his physical decline, Hawking made groundbreaking contributions to theoretical physics, particularly in black hole theory. His 1988 book, A Brief History of Time, became a global bestseller, making complex science accessible to millions.

Confined to a wheelchair and speaking through a computerized voice system, Hawking remained a prominent scientist and public figure for decades. He defied all odds, living for over 50 years after his diagnosis.

Lesson: A strong will and intellectual curiosity can overcome even the most severe limitations.

5. Malala Yousafzai: The Voice of Education

Malala Yousafzai was born in 1997 in Pakistan's Swat Valley. Her father, an educator, instilled in her a love for learning. When the Taliban took control of the region, they banned girls' education, but Malala refused to comply.

At just 11 years old, she began writing a blog for the BBC, detailing life under Taliban rule and advocating for girls' education. Her activism brought her international attention but also made her a target.

In 2012, Malala was shot in the head by a Taliban gunman while riding a bus home from school. Miraculously, she survived and was flown to the UK for treatment. Instead of silencing her, the attack amplified her voice.

Malala co-authored her memoir, I Am Malala, and became the youngest-ever Nobel Peace Prize laureate at 17. She continues to advocate for education worldwide through the Malala Fund.

Lesson: Courage and conviction can challenge oppression and inspire global change.

5 Stories Based On Indians From Which We Can Learn

1.Mahatma Gandhi: The Father of Non-Violent Resistance

Mohandas Karamchand Gandhi, born in 1869 in Porbandar, Gujarat, led India to independence through his philosophy of non-violence (Ahimsa) and truth (Satyagraha).

Educated as a lawyer in London, Gandhi initially struggled to establish his career. A turning point came during his time in South Africa, where he experienced racial discrimination firsthand. This experience galvanized him into action, and he began organizing campaigns for civil rights.

Returning to India in 1915, Gandhi became the leader of the Indian National Congress. He organized non-violent movements such as the Non-Cooperation Movement, the Salt March, and the Quit India Movement, inspiring millions to resist British colonial rule peacefully.

Despite facing imprisonment and personal sacrifices, Gandhi remained steadfast in his belief in non-violence and unity among India's diverse communities. His life ended tragically when he was assassinated in 1948, but his legacy continues to inspire movements for justice worldwide.

Lesson: Non-violence and moral courage can drive profound societal change.

2. Dr. A.P.J. Abdul Kalam: The People's President

Avul Pakir Jainulabdeen Abdul Kalam, born in 1931 in Rameswaram, Tamil Nadu, rose from humble beginnings to become one of India's most respected scientists and the 11th President of India.

Coming from a modest background, Kalam sold newspapers as a child to support his family. His curiosity and hard work led him to study aerospace engineering. He joined the Indian Space Research Organisation (ISRO) and played a pivotal role in developing India's first satellite launch vehicle, SLV-3.

Kalam later contributed to India's nuclear program, earning him the title "Missile Man of India." In 2002, he became President, focusing on youth empowerment, education, and technology. Despite his scientific achievements, he lived a simple life and remained a humble advocate for students.

Kalam passed away in 2015 while delivering a lecture to students, embodying his lifelong dedication to knowledge and service.

Lesson: Hard work, humility, and a commitment to knowledge can lead to greatness.

3. Kalpana Chawla: India's Space Pioneer

Kalpana Chawla, born in 1961 in Karnal, Haryana, became the first woman of Indian origin to travel to space.

Chawla showed an early interest in aeronautics, often drawing airplanes in her notebooks. She pursued engineering at Punjab Engineering College before moving to the United States for advanced studies in aerospace engineering.

In 1997, she joined NASA and flew on her first mission aboard the Space Shuttle Columbia. Her work as a mission specialist and her determination to excel in a male-dominated field earned her immense respect.

In 2003, on her second mission, tragedy struck when the Space Shuttle Columbia disintegrated during re-entry, killing all seven crew members. Chawla's legacy endures as an inspiration for women and aspiring scientists across the globe.

Lesson: Passion and determination can break barriers and inspire generations.

4. Ratan Tata: The Visionary Industrialist

Ratan Tata, born in 1937, transformed the Tata Group into a global powerhouse while maintaining a commitment to ethics and philanthropy.

Raised by his grandmother after his parents' divorce, Tata studied architecture at Cornell University and later attended Harvard Business School. He joined the Tata Group in 1961, starting on the shop floor of Tata Steel.

As chairman of the group from 1991 to 2012, Tata expanded its global reach by acquiring companies like Jaguar Land Rover and Tetley. He also launched the Tata Nano, the world's most affordable car, demonstrating his focus on serving the common man.

Tata is equally known for his philanthropy, dedicating a significant portion of the group's profits to education, healthcare, and rural development. Despite his wealth and achievements, he remains humble and down-to-earth.

Lesson: Leadership rooted in ethics and a commitment to the greater good creates enduring success.

5. Dr. B.R. Ambedkar: The Architect of Modern India

Born in 1891 into a Dalit family, Bhimrao Ramji Ambedkar faced intense caste discrimination from an early age. Despite these challenges, he became a leading scholar, social reformer, and the principal architect of the Indian Constitution.

Ambedkar earned degrees from prestigious institutions like Columbia University and the London School of Economics. He returned to India determined to fight for the rights of the oppressed. His work as a lawyer, writer, and politician laid the foundation for social equality in India.

As the chairman of the drafting committee of the Constitution, Ambedkar ensured provisions for social justice, equality, and individual freedoms. He also championed women's rights and labor reforms.

In his later years, Ambedkar converted to Buddhism, inspiring millions of Dalits to follow suit as a means to escape the caste system. He remains a symbol of resilience and justice.

Lesson: *Knowledge, perseverance, and a commitment to justice can dismantle systemic inequalities.*

5 Poems From Which We Can Learn Something

1. Resilience and Overcoming Challenges

*"Through the storm, the winds will howl,
The darkness deep, the skies will scowl.
Yet in your heart, the fire will glow,
A seed of strength begins to grow.
        Each stumble shapes your steady stride,
Each tear becomes your strength inside.
Rise with scars, but stand with pride,
For life's true victors never hide."*

2. The Power of Self-Belief

*"Within your soul, a voice resides,
A whisper soft, where courage hides.
It speaks of dreams, of goals untold,
It dares your heart to break the mold.
        Believe in you, for none else can
Unlock the strength that makes the plan.
Your path is yours, no need to borrow—
The seeds of today bloom hope for tomorrow."*

3. Growth and Transformation

*"A caterpillar crawls, confined by ground,
Yet in its heart, new wings are found.
Through patience, trials, the chrysalis holds,
Till one fine day, the sky unfolds.

So too, we shed our layers past,
To reach the dreams we've built to last.
Through change, our truest selves are seen,
Transformed by time, reborn, serene."*

4. Mindfulness and Living in the Moment

*"A fleeting breeze, a golden ray,
The simple joys of each new day.
The sunlit path, the whispering trees,
The present moment sets you free.
　　No need to chase what lies ahead,
Or mourn the days that long have fled.
Each breath you take, each step you tread,
Is life itself, where now is fed."*

5. Relationships and Human Connection

*"A hand to hold, a heart to share,
The weight we carry feels less rare.
In kindness flows the bonds we weave,
In love and trust, we can believe.
　　No one stands alone in strife,
We're tied by threads that shape a life.
Together stronger, together whole,
Our hearts entwined, one beating soul."

20 Quotes From Which We Can Learn Something

On Resilience and Challenges

"Our greatest glory is not in never falling, but in rising every time we fall." – Confucius

"Do not judge me by my success, judge me by how many times I fell down and got back up again." – Nelson Mandela

"The world breaks everyone, and afterward, many are strong at the broken places." – Ernest Hemingway

On Self-Belief and Confidence

"Believe you can and you're halfway there." – Theodore Roosevelt

"You are braver than you believe, stronger than you seem, and smarter than you think." – A.A. Milne

"Don't wait. The time will never be just right." – Napoleon Hill

On Growth and Transformation

"Change is the end result of all true learning." – Leo Buscaglia

"What lies behind us and what lies before us are tiny matters compared to what lies within us." – Ralph Waldo Emerson

"The only way to make sense out of change is to plunge into it, move with it, and join the dance." – Alan Watts

On Mindfulness and Living in the Present

"Be happy for this moment. This moment is your life." – Omar Khayyam

"The best way to capture moments is to pay attention. This is how we cultivate mindfulness." – Jon Kabat-Zinn

"Yesterday is history, tomorrow is a mystery, today is a gift—that's why it's called the present." – Eleanor Roosevelt

On Relationships and Connection

"The most important thing in life is to learn how to give out love and to let it come in." – Morrie Schwartz

"In the sweetness of friendship let there be laughter, and sharing of pleasures." – Kahlil Gibran

"Alone we can do so little; together we can do so much." – Helen Keller

On Success and Ambition

"Success is not final, failure is not fatal: It is the courage to continue that counts." – Winston Churchill

"Strive not to be a success, but rather to be of value." – Albert Einstein

"Opportunities don't happen. You create them." – Chris Grosser

On Life and Perspective

"Do what you can, with what you have, where you are." – Theodore Roosevelt

"Life isn't about finding yourself. It's about creating yourself." – George Bernard Shaw

Thanks

A Note of Gratitude to My Readers

Dear Reader,

Thank you for embarking on this journey with me. Writing this book has been an act of reflection, vulnerability, and hope—and your decision to read it means more to me than words can express.

In a world filled with endless distractions and choices, you've chosen to invest your time in these pages. That is a gift I deeply cherish. My goal has always been to connect, inspire, and empower, and knowing that you're here, exploring these ideas, gives this work its true meaning.

Your openness to learn, grow, and transform is what makes this journey worthwhile. Every word written here was with you in mind—your struggles, aspirations, and potential. I hope this book offers you not just guidance but also a sense of companionship and encouragement as you navigate your unique path.

If these words have sparked even a small change in your perspective or ignited a new idea, then I have accomplished what I set out to do.

Thank you for your trust and for allowing me to be a part of your story. May this book be a stepping stone to the extraordinary life you're destined to create.

With heartfelt gratitude,
[Kushal Gupta]

www.ingramcontent.com/pod-product-compliance
Lightning Source LLC
Chambersburg PA
CBHW061346160726
47995CB00001B/190